Advance Praise for
# DOUBLE DUTCHING IN MY OWN SKIN

"This represents an important contribution to understanding the intersectionality of intra-racial gender norming and skin tone interpersonal appraisals as ingredients for adverse black-on-black interaction. The author's auto-ethnographic contribution thoroughly delivered the nature of a Black Woman's war within. It is extremely rare to advance discussions of colorism beyond the "halo-effect" to discover intrasexual social conflict. Kudos to the author for the courage to delve into the painful reality of intra-racial and gendered skin tone victimization.

—Dr. Steven R. Cureton, Professor and Chair of The University of North Carolina at Greensboro's Sociology Department"

In Double Dutching In My Own Skin: A Soulful Narrative on Colorism, Dr. LaWanda Simpkins takes us on a powerful, storied journey through her lived experience as a light-skinned Black woman. From her lens - one often considered one of color privilege - she asks the important question, "Can a person be privileged for the same identity that they are oppressed for?" and gets our heads spinning in search of the answer. This thought-provoking auto ethnographic exploration is empowering, sincere, brilliant, and a necessary contribution to the Colorism lexicon.

—Dawn N. Hicks Tafari, Ph.D., Associate Professor of Education, Winston-Salem State University Author of "Whose World is This?": A Composite Counter story of Black Male Elementary School Teachers as Hip-Hop Other fathers"

# Double Dutching in My Own Skin

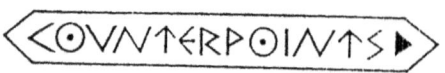

# Counterpoints Primers

Shirley R. Steinberg
*Series Editor*

Vol. 39

LaWanda M. Simpkins

# Double Dutching in My Own Skin

## A Soulful Narrative on Colorism

PETER LANG
New York · Berlin · Bruxelles · Chennai · Lausanne · Oxford

Library of Congress Cataloging-in-Publication Control Number: 2023030391

Bibliographic information published by the Deutsche Nationalbibliothek.
The German National Library lists this publication in the German National Bibliography; detailed bibliographic data is available on the Internet at http://dnb.d-nb.de.

Cover design by Cover art by Xavier Carrington

ISSN 2832-9597 (print) ISSN 2832-9600 (online)
ISBN 9781636673097 (paperback)
ISBN 9781636673103 (ebook)
ISBN 9781636673110 (epub)
DOI 10.3726/ b21027

© 2024 Peter Lang Group AG, Lausanne
Published by Peter Lang Publishing Inc., New York, USA
info@peterlang.com - www.peterlang.com

All rights reserved.
All parts of this publication are protected by copyright.
Any utilization outside the strict limits of the copyright law, without the permission of the publisher, is forbidden and liable to prosecution.
This applies in particular to reproductions, translations, microfilming, and storage and processing in electronic retrieval systems.

This publication has been peer reviewed.

To Little Me. Glad you finally spoke up.

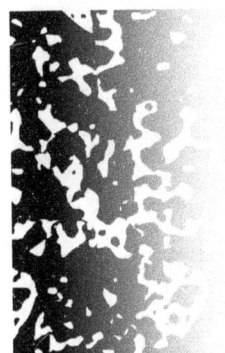

# Contents

Preface ..................................................................xi

1. Down with Fraggle Rock: Freckles, Red Hair, and Stones..................................................................1
   Introduction ..........................................................1
      Goals................................................................8

2. There's Nobody New under the Sun: Some Are Told They Can Play Outside and Some Are Warned Against It............................................11
   Introduction ........................................................11
   Race....................................................................13
      Biological Origins..............................................14
      Time Overview..................................................15
      Critical Race Theory .........................................17
   Racism................................................................18
      Internalized Racism ..........................................20
   Colorism.............................................................21
      Early Stages of Colorism ..................................22
      Passing...........................................................23
      Too Light—Too Dark.........................................24
      Which Black Is Beautiful..................................26

    Family ....................................................................... 27
    Conclusion ............................................................... 30

3. **Skin Tone and Attitude: Color Stratification Amongst Black Actresses** ........................ 33
    Introduction .......................................................... 34
    Film Industry ........................................................ 36
    Mammy, Sapphire, and Jezebel ...................... 37
        Mammy .............................................................. 37
        Sapphire ............................................................. 38
        Jezebel ................................................................ 39
    Trinary Thinking .................................................. 41
    Stereotypes and Reality ...................................... 43
        Light Skinned Objects .................................... 44
    My Fantasy and Reality ...................................... 45
    School Daze ........................................................... 45
    Conclusion ............................................................. 48

4. **Tales of a Melanated Sistah: Journaling through Colorism** .............................................. 51
    Introduction .......................................................... 51
    Family ...................................................................... 53
        Why Would I Do This to My Kids? ............... 55
        Not Wanting to Be an AKA ........................... 58
        Even Tanning Can't Take the Pain Away ..... 61
    Self-Actualization—Proving My Blackness ....... 63
        She Is a REAL Sistah ....................................... 65
    Divided Perception: They Like Him Better ...... 67
        I Am Light Skin Darn It! ................................ 70
        #teamlightskin ................................................ 72
    Conclusion ............................................................. 73

5. **You Can't Stay in the Past So How Do We Move Forward: Education as a Form of Liberation** ............................................................. 75
    Golden ..................................................................... 79
    Liberation through Education ............................ 80
        Community ....................................................... 81
        Culturally Relevant Classrooms ................... 82
        Media Responsibility ..................................... 84
        Intergroup Dialogue ...................................... 86
        Journaling ......................................................... 87
    Conclusion ............................................................. 88

**Bibliography** ..................................................... **91**

**Index** ................................................................... **99**

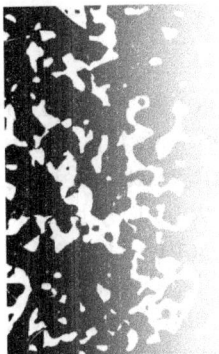

# Preface

Patiently, I sat in his office. With my heart beating and hands trembling I took my first deep breath before I began sharing my work, my passion with my classmates and professor. As I started, I stumbled over my words because my words were my thoughts, and my thoughts were intimate to me. I was nervous! Saying them out loud made them real. Writing them down would make them a permanent document, something that other people could read. As I shared with them what had been the story of my life my eyes swole with tears and my face began to turn pink. I hate that my skin always shows all.

I wondered why everyone was silent. As they left the classroom all my classmates patted me on my back. I'm still not certain if the pat was saying, "job well done" or "hang in there", but nevertheless they all did it; every single one of them. The next day a classmate and dear friend called to check on me. She wanted to make sure that I was okay. I uncomfortably laughed at her and asked what did she

think was wrong with me? She got so quiet. Her silence on the phone unnerved me. With a steady calm voice (like she was being gentle with me) she stated, "your eyes were red and swollen with tears last night." In my uncomfortable state I laughed it off. I told her "Oh that was just allergies." I knew my eyes had swollen with tears, but I thought it was just a little bit. Who would really cry in class I said to her. I began talking about something else all while having many thoughts. Why was she in my personal space? Did she not know I was melting on the inside? I wanted her to back off me, but I knew she was going to continue to push. I wondered if she picked up on all the things that she said because she knew me well or was it just that obvious to everyone.

The next week one of my classmates approached me before class got started. He wanted to make sure that I did not think that he was patronizing me by patting me on my back. I assured him that I had not put any more thought into it, which was partially untrue. I had thought about it but not necessarily in the way that he had believed that I had. I wondered if he too saw what my dear friend had seen. Apparently, he had. I had no idea that my topic was going to affect me like this. On our first day of class my professor said my book should be an extension of me. He told me to write about the very thing that was important and deep in my soul. He said write about what I am passionate about and not to be bound by structure and tradition. So, I took his advice not considering that in doing so it was going to affect me the way that it did last week.

I knew I had chosen the right topic, but until sharing it with my classmates, I felt that it was important to keep my personal life as far away from my work as possible. After all, I planned to write about colorism as a light skinned Black woman, who, according to the idea of colorism, have been privileged by my skin. What voice could I really give to the situation? Furthermore, who would care to listen?

Every person in the room, including my professor suggested that I do a personal narrative. I began to get very defensive. I thought who me, are these people crazy? They wanted me to talk about colorism from my perspective. Were they really suggesting that I spend pages upon pages talking about the life of a light skinned Black woman? No way! That was unheard of. Should my book not give voice, freedom, even vengeance to those people who are darker than I? Are they not the ones who deserve to be heard? Through the constant back and forth conversation all I could think of was how badly I wanted that moment to end. Maybe then I would have time to come up with all the many reasons that they were wrong about my voice being important and I was right about remaining silent. Maybe I could possibly come up with all the ways in which I could convince them that approaching my work from another angle would perhaps be more meaningful.

Then the strangest thing happened. I realized they were right. My voice could be heard. Maybe it should be heard. I felt the urgency to include my life. I felt that it was an essential piece to not only the ever-evolving development of my work, but also to myself. For the first time ever, I really began to embrace the idea of a personal narrative and the added benefit that it would give to my readers. As I thought about it even more, I also thought about how liberating it might be. I pondered a little longer on how I would map out my first literary masterpiece (in my mind at least).

The project was so big I didn't know where to begin. I started with my safe place, journaling. I knew it would lead to something. I knew that writing would help me, explore, discover, and yes maybe even overcome my fears, complexities and anxieties about colorism. I wanted to do this all while creating a work that would make my future self proud. Like any work of fine art, I stared at the blank canvas and wondered what it would one day become. I knew my work would be special to me. Not perfect but maybe perfect in my eyes. I knew this was just the beginning. I could feel that. I had no idea what

I was about to truly get myself into. I hoped that it would touch the lives of those who read it. I hoped it would touch my life as well. With excitement and fear I thought "here goes nothing and everything all wrapped up in one."

Signed Me spring 2010

Many years ago, I wrote the words you just read. Now years later I still share in some of these same fears but not in the same way that I once did. I'm older now, wiser, and more mature. I know enough to believe that my voice is important and that by using it I am not taking away space from others who may believe differently from me. I also know enough now to know that the topic of colorism needs to be heard in every space and in every way. Thank you for sharing this space and time with me.

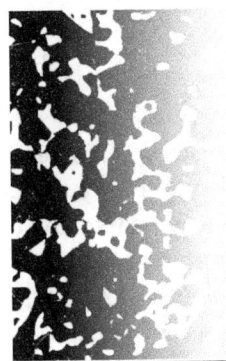

CHAPTER ONE

# Down with Fraggle Rock: Freckles, Red Hair, and Stones

## Introduction

As I stand in the circle with one rock on my shoulder while looking at the rock on the girl's shoulder in front of me, I am steaming on the inside. I cannot believe that I am standing "here" again. As the other kid's chant "fight, fight, fight" I ball my fist up in anticipation of what seemed like a regular occurrence in my childhood, another fight. "Hit that yellow banana "or "Slap that rock off of that tar baby's shoulder" gets louder and louder before finally one of us gets up enough courage to take the first swing. The fight starts, finishes and ends, only to happen again real soon. I can't tell you how many times this happened in my childhood, but what I can say is I won some and I lost some. Now that I am older, I realize that even the ones that I won I really lost.

These fights took place during my childhood, and if you would have asked either of us why we were really fighting I know that we could not have

told you the truth. All I knew was I was angry because she was angry, and, equally so, she was angry because I was angry. The sad part is, we were fighting a fight that had begun many years before we were even born; yet we were both fighting as if our lives depended on it. I don't even remember the people that I fought, but I do remember the intensity that I felt when I was doing it. I physically fought to stand my ground in my neighborhood, just to make it known that simply because I was light, high yellow, red or any other demeaning adjective they used to describe me, that I was still Black, and nobody could ever take that away from me. "Light-skinned Black women face the challenge of not being accepted by others in their race as well as feeling guilty or shameful about the unfair advantages they are said to have" (Glenn, 2009, p. 34). As a child, I would not have been able to articulate it in that way, but I knew what I was fighting for, I just did not really know why I was fighting for it. Although I was tired of the fights, I welcomed them on every occasion because it gave me the opportunity to "prove" myself.

I would be foolish to think that all my fights stemmed solely because of my complexion; however, from the comments that I heard before, during and after the altercations, I know that many of them did. I was able to grow up and learn how to ignore such comments as "you think you are cute because you are light skin" but unfortunately everyone does not get beyond these thoughts, or even beyond making the comments themselves for that matter. They show up in different ways and spaces and often times very subtly.

The need to prove your "Blackness" was very real for me growing up as a child. I grew up during an era where to be Black was to be beautiful. "The Blacker the berry the sweeter the juice" was a common catch phrase during the 1990s. Those who were not so dark may not have always been esteemed as being sweet. This translated directly to how "Black" they were. The lighter you were the less Black people saw you as if to say that being Black was an adjective versus a noun.

As a child, I did not fully understand why kids could hate me because of my skin tone alone. I grew up just like them, middle class (probably more like poor) with lots of hopes and dreams and no clear vision to get where I wanted to go. My mom was a single mother, we moved just about every year of my life, we never had a car growing up, I wore my sister's secondhand clothes if they fit and at times my shoes had holes in them, but yet I was the center of most kid's envy. For the life of me I could never understand why.

I vividly remember in the sixth grade being told in the bathroom by a girl that on the last day of school I better not come because I was going to get jumped. I was terrified and went home fearful and afraid to go back the next day. When I told my sister and now brother-in-law, they told me that I better go and if I ran from that one threat that I would be running for the rest of my life which was very solid advice. Even though I had gotten into many fights in my neighborhood something about a fight at school seemed petrifying. This was probably because I had more to lose, because I was a cheerleader and on student council. I went to school. The advice they gave me was great because I got threatened many times in my life after that and much like the threat from sixth grade, the people never came through, thank God. I remember timidly asking the girl why I would get jumped and the answer she gave was the one that haunted my existence: "because you think you are cute because you are light skinned." Although I did not have to physically fight that day in middle school, the emotional fight left an everlasting scar on my life. So much so that I am writing this book.

Growing up with light skin in the South taught me a valuable lesson: it doesn't matter if your color is not seen as an asset to you, if others around you feel that it is, then it is possible that they may have deep feelings concerning it and may act accordingly. When young girls said that I thought I was cute because I was light skinned, or "when I first met you, I thought you were stuck up because of your complexion but now that I know you, I realize you are cool" what I really heard them say was that they believed that I thought that I was better than them simply because of my skin tone. I never thought this. Unfortunately, this belief holds true for many people within minority communities.

Now almost 30 years after my childhood fights, I am left with the invisible scars of what my shade meant to others as a child. I now have children of my own and I think about what their complexion might mean to others. More importantly what their complexion might mean to them. Through life experiences I have become aware of why children made the comments that they made many years ago and am ready to confront and challenge the ideas and mindsets that several people within the African American community hold when it comes to race and various complexions.

When a person is discriminated against, treated differently, shunned, or made to be an outcast because of the shade of their skin, they are experiencing the brutal effects of intra-racism. As one might believe intra-racism, also known as inter-racism, internalized racism and, or colorism are all subsidiaries of racism, except it is found in majority among members of Black and Brown communities. The standard definition of colorism is a systematic preference for lightness that stems from the larger and more potent system of racism. Many have internalized this racism so deeply, that they can no longer recognize colorism and racism for what they are, and instead see them simply as individual taste (Hunter, 2005) versus the chronic disorder that it truly is. In the medical world a chronic disorder is defined as a human health condition or disease that is persistent or otherwise long lasting in its effects. The term *chronic* is usually applied when the course of the disease lasts for more than three months (M. Williams, Teasdale, Segal, & Kabat-Zinn, 2007). It is apparent to see that colorism has existed longer than this.

Most of what is written and documented on colorism would lead one to believe that people who are Black but have a lighter hue have better spouses/partners, children, employment, social organizations and education. Overall, it is presumed that a Black person with light skin will have a better quality of life (Burton, Bonilla-Silva, Ray, Budkelew, & Freeman, 2010; Glenn, 2009; Golden, 2004; Hunter, 2005; Russell, Wilson & Hall, 1992; Wilder & Cain, 2010). This belief is systemic from the early influence of color preferences that originated during slavery (Henderson, 2002) and has been held as "truth" over time. The word "better" gives me grief, but nevertheless it is how light-skinned women are spoken of.

The studies that have been done conclusively state that life would be better simply by having lighter skin. This information is typically formulated through narrative inquiry; where by both dark-skinned and light-skinned women have been interviewed. Also, quantitative research via surveys has also been used to capture this information (Glenn, 2009). What has yet to be seen is an autobiographical study of a light skin Black woman that could challenge these said norms. I am certain that this is missing for due cause. In the conundrum of internalized racism, intra-racism or colorism, a lighter complexion Black person is supposed to benefit from having lighter skin, thus exploring the idea and possibly learning that this may not be true would disrupt the idea of privilege that many argue factually comes with having a lighter complexion.

When I was in my twenties I decided to "do the work" of self-healing as it relates to colorism. I knew what I had read and saw but I also knew what I had experienced. I initially sought out to do my work the same way that I had seen it done. I wanted to talk about the hurt that darker hue women experienced as it relates to colorism, but something happened when I began to share this story. One, as a lighter hue Black woman it was not my story to share but secondly, and perhaps most important, I too had been the victim of the brutal effects of racism and colorism. You see, I am Black woman, and outside of the paradigm of internalized racism, I am seen as Black. Not light or dark, just Black. I am not negating that historically lighter skin Black people did not and perhaps do receive a set of privileges within the Black community, but what I can I say for certain is that I have not escaped the ugly fatalities of racism because my skin is lighter. And as far as colorism goes, I have had to apologize for the hurt that others have felt because of someone who may have had my complexion. I have been sexualized and minimized and, like this story began, had to fight to prove that I was Black enough. It is something to be said about fitting in but not fitting in enough.

This uncomfortable truth led me to seek more knowledge about what I was experiencing. I started by reading the few books that were out at the time on the topic. One of which was a nonfiction work about a Black woman growing up in the South and her journey of being the *wrong color* (she was dark skinned) and how that shaped her life. On one hand I was very sorry for what she felt and experienced growing up. On another hand I was in disbelief and frustrated that she could blame so much of what had gone wrong in her life on the complexion of another Black woman's skin. In her eyes, she literally stood back in the presence of light skinned women. This idea troubled me deeply.

In 2011 D. Channsin Berry and Bill Duke directed *Dark Girls,* a documentary which focuses on colorism from the perspective of darker complexion women. In 2014 Oprah utilized her platform to discuss the issue. News correspondents on CNN have also tackled the topic. I was very excited to watch all of these and much like the book I read, these documentaries share personal stories of how colorism has affected the lives of many. Although I believe each of the works to be eloquently done, in many ways they reinforced the master narrative in the

Black community which asserts that dark is "bad" and light is "good."

It is this master narrative that prompted what you will read in this book. I offer a counter narrative of what it is like to have lighter skin while navigating through the color complex. Presumably I have the *right color* skin which should have afforded me more opportunities in life. I write this work with confidence but not without fear because I am telling a story from a side that has not quite been told yet.

Because I am an African American woman who has been socialized in a Black community in North Carolina, which is in the southern hemisphere of the United States of America, I have chosen to focus my book on the issue of colorism within my country. Choosing to focus solely on America does not imply that the effects of color stratification do not exist within other minority communities or countries. Nor does it imply that their experiences could not be comparable to people within the Black community here. I am simply speaking from the perspective that I understand.

In this work I explore the phenomenon of colorism from the perspective of being a light skinned African American woman. I offer that the traditional definition of colorism, which is a form of internalized racism and the belief that light skin provides privilege over dark skin within a set marginalized group (Glenn, 2009; Golden, 2004; Russell et al., 1992) should in fact read the colorism is internalized racism. To understand this complicated idea, I examine the social construction of race, Black Feminist Thought (BFT) and Critical Race Theory (CRT) while engaging in an autoethnographic project to explore this subject.

Personal experiences and memories are shared throughout this work. In fact, there is an entire chapter dedicated to this. I understand that I have an obligation as the author of this work to provide accurate accounts of colorism as I have experienced them. I take this responsibility very seriously. Even being true I understand that there are memories in my life which include others whom, because of the unambiguous role in my life, were unable to be disguised. The use of pseudo names would not have changed their role in my stories. Whereas I do not find the stories to be offensive in any way that could embarrass them, I still offer my apologies to them in advance for sharing something that perhaps they may not have wanted shared and, or did not know I processed it in the way that I did. I also offer assurance, if there is any doubt, that they are not a personal project to me. Their life experiences simply coincided with my own.

### Goals

My goals are very clear and simple. By examining the everyday narratives that have taken place around me before and throughout my writing process I explore how research coincides with my lived experiences. I also use films as a form of content analysis to explore the collective identity of Black women. Because movies are very instrumental in how Black women are viewed and perceived by society, I will utilize them to discuss how they help form and perpetuate the master narrative concerning colorism.

Drawing upon the existing research on internalized racism I explore the variations of colorism as documented juxtaposed to my actual lived experiences as a light-skin African American woman. This autobiographical work is known in research as autoethnography (Chang, 2008; Denzin, 1997; Ellis, 2004). It is supported by the existing literature, but the most important component of the study is the researcher. This type of research pushes scholars to a new level of understanding and develops a depth in your soul that can only be created through experiencing the process. As Poulos (2009) offers, "There is something about getting lost, and then getting 'un-lost,' that changes you" (p. 52). Autoethnography certainly has the ability to change you. It is important to emphasize that it is not completely autobiographical but rather a harmonious balance between research on internalized racism/intra-racism/colorism, intertwined with my lived experience. Overall, it is about how the researcher fits into the bigger context of the cultural issue.

With the increasing conversations and debates concerning race and shades of skin I feel that I am never able to separate myself from my work. We are what we become, and we become what we are. It is this constant immersion and the ability to interchangeably penetrate circles that I have chosen to write in this autoethnographic way. My personal childhood experiences, my upbringing, my high school years, my college experience and now my adult life have all had traces of colorism. Not only am I constantly surrounded by the idea, but also, I believe that everyone is, whether they recognize or choose to acknowledge it or not. While I fervently believe this, I am aware that not all Black people hold the belief that colorism still exists. I often speak of this experience with sistahs (other Black women) who are a browner hue and to my surprise they usually do not understand nor are they fully aware that such division is taking place among Black women. This is because those people who are either very light or very dark are the ones who usually feel the effects of colorism; those in the middle tend to be "safe" (Golden, 2004; Hunter, 2005). "It doesn't matter if we are light or if we are dark, we all feel like we're not enough or who we are because we are always being pursued, attacked, or rejected because of what we look like" (Golden, 2004, p. 108). Those who are in the "middle" may be protected from the intra social effects of colorism but are not protected by the inter effects of the social structure of skin tone stratification.

The titles of my chapters were influenced by the most evocative memories I had, either while writing the chapter or a memory I had which related to the chapter. For example, this first chapter, *Down with Fraggle Rock,* was a very popular television show when I was a young. Among the silly names that I was called that had to deal with me looking

"yellow" I was also called names that had to deal with my features. As a child, I had considerable tints of red in my hair, which I wished to go away, now I wish to come back. I also had freckles on my face, which I still have. Because of this I was teased. Now that I look back on the show, red fraggle was actually very cute, but during my childhood I never felt cute when I was called that name. Somehow, I feel that when kids called me this they were not thinking of me as cute.

Being open about myself in this work that I am producing is my highest priority. Authenticity is acting in accordance with one's true self. It is in this way that one is being honest and sincere (Henry, Kernis, & Goldman, as cited in Fleeson & Wilt, 2010, p. 1354). In a world of confusion, chaos and lies, being true to oneself, their work, and their commitment to tell their truth is invaluable. Overall, I plan to tell a story. One, which may not be completely unfamiliar or may be familiar to others, but one that I hope will ultimately generate new ideas, meanings and ways of knowing. I want my work to be a part of the everyday barber or beauty shop conversations. There are multiple and competing truths. This book is simply my truth.

CHAPTER TWO

# There's Nobody New under The Sun: Some Are Told They Can Play Outside and Some Are Warned Against It

**Introduction**

I was never told that I could not go outside and play in the sun. In fact, as a young child I was encouraged to do so. The only requirement that I had was to put sunscreen on so that I would not burn, and yes, you guessed it, if you are a child of the 80's or before, to be back inside before the streetlights came on. Being a child during that time on the surface was seemingly easy.

Even with that being true, from as early as I can remember my complexion has always been a topic of discussion. From childhood fights to middle school arguments, high school popularity contest of who was least liked (I was ranked in the top three along with two other light skinned girls) to college and adult years; I can truly say that I do not have a memory in my life where my complexion has not been on the forefront of most discussions.

This underlying force to talk about my complexion is not because of who I am or what my shade of color is, but rather is part of the oppressive nature of colorism. Colorism, which is the belief and practice that light skin, provides privilege over dark skin within a set marginalized group (Glenn, 2009; Golden, 2004; Hunter, 2005; Russell et al., 1992) has been a destructive force within minority communities around the world. Dormant beneath the struggles of people of color is a deeper issue that torments their existence. Colorism is considered one of the most deeply rooted secrets amongst African Americans and other minority groups that destroy communities. It positions people within the same race against each other based off the shade of their skin. This internal fight is both pointless and harmful. No matter how great the difference of shade, the people fighting are still minorities, and are treated and seen as such by those who choose to use their power as oppressors. Someone once said to me that things are only oppressive if you allow them to be. I think that's part truth, more wishful thinking.

The belief that one group of people is better than another group of people solely based on skin tone is the core value of racism (Gallagher, 2009; Graves, 2005). This idea has served as the root of much self-hatred, loathing, and division amongst many marginalized populations. In this chapter I explain colorism. I trace its evolution through race and racism in America. I identify the key components of the phenomenon by comprehensively defining its meaning and identifying the many names it is called according to the leading scholars in the field. I also discuss who is affected by it and finally how it has plagued the African American community.

Before I examine colorism however, I must discuss the social construction of race and racism in America. Without either of the two, colorism would not exist.

## Race

On April 4, 1968 America was changed forever. One of the most influential Black leaders of our time was gunned down and killed in Memphis, Tennessee while simply standing on Lorraine Motel balcony with his colleagues. Prior to this day Dr. Martin Luther King, Jr. gave one of his most electrifying speeches, which eerily talked, about his final days on earth (Dyson, 2008). The man who took Dr. King's life, James Earl Ray, pleaded guilty and was sentenced to 99 years in prison. Immediately after being sentenced Ray retracted his earlier confession of killing Dr. King and spent the remainder of his life unsuccessfully trying to prove his innocence. Many people believe that Ray was not Dr. King's assassin. In fact, King's own family agreed. There are multiple conspiracy theories surrounding Dr. King's death, but most would agree that he died for, in the name of and because of race.

Race in America has defined the way in which we move breathe and exist in our western culture. Oxford American Dictionary (2011) very simply defined race as one of the main groups that humans can be dived into according to their physical differences, for example the color of their skin. In 2023 this definition still holds true. Race is everything that we see but is truly everything that we are not. In this modern time, many people try to define race according to whom they believe they are, but the truth of the matter is race has been and is defined by those who have power. It does not matter how we see ourselves when it comes to race, it is how others perceive and receive us. Although race is very simply defined as people having common origin and is socially constructed, the effects of it, especially speaking historically, are very real. Thinking about how race came to exist in America is truly complicated. Race means something completely different in other parts of the world.

**Biological Origins**

There is no biological evidence which justifies how we classify people in races yet "most Americans still believe in the concept of race the way they believe in the law of gravity -they believe in it without even knowing what it is they believe in" (Graves, 2005, p. xxv). In this country we look at a person's skin, hair, nose, eyes, language and body to identify them. By looking at features we are supposed to automatically understand who they are and how we should respond to them. Furthermore, our lived experiences inform us on how we should act according to the visual characteristics that may be similar to that of another person with the same characteristics. This notion of identifying individuals by gazing at them leads to a shallow and meaningless way of categorizing individuals. It does not take into account the socio-economic status, the religious views, the personal sexual orientation, the educational background and on a simple level the personal beliefs of individuals. In trying to discern who a person truly is race is the last social identifier that anyone should ever view. Unfortunately, our American history has taught us that it is the first way and, in many instances, the only way that people identify and are identified.

Race is very real and dominant in America. Simplistic notions of it being a "social construction" do not equal or balance out the everlasting effects that it has on society. Race is so deeply ingrained that it will take twice as many years to undo the deflating value that it has placed on human life as it took to create the unlawful hierarchy. Race is complicated. It is very real. In the ever-true words of Cornell West, "Race Matters" (2001), and while many Americans believe that everyone has "equal" access and the abilities to live the same lives, many others understand the falsehood in this idea.

It has been written that race originated as a way to categorize humankind. In the matter of race, all persons who are not white are considered to be the "other" and are therefore classified as inferior. In some cases, consequently their lives are considered as such.

> Scholars have noted that race was and continues to be a social construction wielded by White Europeans and Americans to establish social demarcations, elevate the White race, and justify the oppression and exploitation of certain ethnic groups who were presumed to be inferior in intelligence, physicality, morality and culture. (C. Thompson & Carter, 1997, p. 3)

The interest of the dominant culture to perpetuate the false construction or race lies within economic and political benefits that are gained. It is not just the dominant culture, however, that perpetuates the divide and the nuisances of race, which ultimately leads to racism. Hegemony, which is the belief that the dominant cultures ways benefit "you" when in actuality they do not and were never intended to, has been the root of perpetuation of many racial ideas among minority people. Aufderheide and Kampmeir (2008) define minority as a group of people who have less power than the dominant group.

### Time Overview

Trying to pinpoint an exact date when race relations began is very difficult. From the deadly and heart wrenching middle passage, the slave trade, plantation life, share cropping, industrial times, the civil rights movement, the postmodern era and finally to today's society, we understand that race has been around for at least a century. During World War I (1914–1918) noted scholar W. E. B. Dubois wrote "the discovery of personal whiteness among the world's peoples is a very modern thing" (Holt, 1998, p. 71). It was this discovery which ultimately led to racism.

Race became of value when labor markets were unfulfilled. "The West African slave trade and Southern auction blocks treated both Black women's and men's bodies as objects for sale" (Collins, 2005, p. 30). Traders kidnapped Africans and sold them into slavery. History books date back to as early as 1619 to note the first Africans being sold into slavery and 1641 as Massachusetts being the first state to legalize slavery (Finkelman, 2010). By 1863 approximately 10–12 million human beings had been sold into slavery when President Abraham Lincoln passed the Emancipation Proclamation, which was intended to abolish slavery. Although slavery was illegal, it still was very present in the lives of white and Black people.

This declaration to end slavery accelerated the movement to minimize Black value and to propel whiteness as significance. I would be remiss if I did not mention that from 1863 to our current day matters, Black Americans (also typically classified as African Americans) have been exploited, exposed, devalued, humiliated, and mistreated. All of this stems from the social construction of race. "Race has historically been and may still be a significant factor in determining the life chances of Blacks" (Cureton, 2002, p. 49) and although a person's class does shield some African Americans from this harsh historical reality when it truly matters, and even when it doesn't, a person's race will always overshadow anything else.

Race is about dominance and wealth. Race is about whiteness and all that is not that. "Whiteness is everywhere in American culture, but it is very hard to see. As Richard Dyers (1988) argues, "White power secures its dominance by seeming not to be anything in particular" (p. 44). The lack of biological evidence has failed to relinquish the power dynamic of race. The social construction of race illuminates what is real, what is different, what is equal and what is not. Combined together we understand the dynamics of the social component of racism.

**Critical Race Theory**

Critical Race Theory (CRT) is one of the theories which helps us understand the social construction of race and racism in American history. Originally beginning as a movement of legal studies in the early 1970's, it examines race, law, power, and the intersection of each. Derrick Bell and Richard Delgado are noted as the fathers of Critical Race Theory (CRT). Other contributing scholars are Patricia Williams, Kimberle Williams Crenshaw, and Mari Mastuda. Critical race theorists assess social systems and groups. The core ideas suggests that:

(a) Race is a central component of social organizations and systems, including families
(b) Racism is institutionalized-it is an ingrained feature of racialized social systems
(c) Everyone within racialized social systems may contribute to the end reproduction of these systems through social practices and
(d) Racial and ethnic identities, in addition to "the rules, practices, and assignments of prestige power" associated with them, are not fixed entities, but rather they are socially constructed phenomena that are continually being revised on the basis of a group's own self-interests. (Delgado, as cited in Burton et al., 2010, p. 442)

The core principles of CRT illuminate the ways in which race has and continues to be fluid within the American legal and social system. "Derrick Bell argued that civil right advances for Blacks always coincided with changing economic conditions and the self-interest of elite whites" (Delgado & Stefancic, 2001, p. 18). Critical Race Theory focuses on mainstream whiteness and how it continues to play

a role in our lives. At the core, it deals with the oppressive nature of racism in America.

## Racism

The evolution of race ultimately led to the unforgiving system of racialized oppression, commonly known as racism. Although racism is the personal, individual expression of prejudice (Sniderman & Piazza, 1993), it is situated within a larger context of biases that have become the social norm. This normalcy is created so that the white race remains dominant within the American culture. "The entire white identity model is organized around individuals getting to feel good about being white in a non-racist way" (A. Thompson, 2010, p. 15).

Racism has been around for many years within our American culture. Up until most recently with the reemergence of the Black Lives Matter Movement, many people believed that racism did not exist anymore. In fact, some naive people believe that racism would go away if people would simply stop talking about it. "I think that, I don't know—they live too much in the past, if you ask me. Some of 'em do. You know, I think Blacks are more prejudiced against whites than whites are against Blacks" (as cited in Bonilla-Silva, 2006, p. 65) This type of belief is what Eduardo Bonilla-Silva (2006) describes as color-blind racism, racism without race.

In this modern-day racism ethnic biases are believed to be the norm, racism is not bad because it is better than it was in the past, everyone is believed to have the same opportunities in life and worse of all, people do not see color they simply see people. This type of racism has especially been pervasive in the past decade when the first Black President Barack Obama was elected for two terms. Unfortunately, during his term as president, it was documented that many interracial couples were still denied the opportunity to legally marry in some areas of the United States, racial profiling of African Americans by White police officers was still prevalent and Mexican immigrants were still discriminated against in violent ways (Burton et al., 2010). This shows that race and racism are still as ubiquitous today as it has been in prior years. Speight (2006) accounts:

> No one has to call me a derogatory name for me to understand that as an African American I am devalued in this society. Actually, the fact that I have not been called the "N word" (to my face) in 20 years has heightened my awareness of the many other subtle ways that I am demeaned, diminished, constrained, and objectified in our society because of my group identities. (p. 130)

Even with all the evidence and so many personal accounts, heard and unheard, many people claim to not see race anymore. Perhaps worse if they do see it they claim that it no longer matters in today's society. Even after the unjust killings of Black and Brown people at the hands of those who are called to protect and serve, many people fail to realize that race and racism are alive and well in our current society.

Much of how people view race depends greatly upon where they are situated within the racial framework. Whites have the most interest in race because they benefit from it the most. "Since actors racialized as "white"—or as members of the dominant race- receive material benefits from the racial order, they struggle (or passively receive the manifold wages of whiteness) to maintain their privileges" (Bonilla-Silva, 2006, p. 9). Despite this being true the dominance of race cannot be enacted without all races buying into the idea, thus one of the core principles of Critical Race Theory.

Members of the non-majority race are key actors in the institution of race. By internalizing stereotypes and images that certain societal elements have constructed, members of minority groups help to maintain the power of the majority race (Ladson-Billings, 2010). This internalization is known as hegemony as well as cultural imperialism (Adams et al., 2000; Speight, 2006; Young, 2000). When this type of internalization happens instead of questioning stereotypes members of the minority race accept them as the truth.

Being part of a marginalized group causes you to look at life in different ways than a dominant group may not have to. At times this way may possibly cause you to not only focus on yourself, but also others who may *look* like you. Because the negative images of minority groups are reinforced in everyday life and language, unless you are very socially and culturally aware, you will be susceptible to internalizing what is around you. Even in being socially aware "it is possible to overlook something that's in plain view if we don't expect to see it" (Schwalbe, 2008, p. 120). Since negative ideas about marginalized groups are taken for granted and as common knowledge, we do not expect to see anything else. This lack for difference can make it difficult to see that which is before us thus subconsciously embracing it. Furthermore, Gainor (2008) adds that "when the prejudices and misinformation about one's group have been internalized, then spending time with others like oneself can stimulate one's own self-loathing and lead people of the same oppressed group to be suspicious of each other" (p. 236). This type of suspicion can lead to internal turmoil which serves as the root of intra (within) racial issues.

### Internalized Racism

Without the evolution of race, there would be no racism. Racism serves as one form of oppression, which many minorities have internalized, thus owning its harmful effects. "Internalized racism has been referred to as a disease that infects communities of color" (Asanti, as cited in Hipolito-Delgado, 2010, p. 319). Colorism is certainly a form of internalized racism. Speight (2006) explores five forms of oppression, citing the internalization of race as being connected to one of the five areas. She makes a very strong argument which positions this form of internalized oppression to perhaps be the most damaging of them all. The effects of internalized racism have yet to fully be examined. Speight (2006) along with Burton et al. (2010) express the sense of urgency in learning more about this phenomenon. This internalization within the African American community usually manifests itself through colorism. The remainder of this chapter will be dedicated to discussing this concept.

## Colorism

The complexity of race being socially constructed further confounds the idea of colorism, which is the belief and practice that light skin provides privilege over dark skin within a set marginalized group (Glenn, 2009; Golden, 2004; Hunter, 2005; Russell et al., 1992). Race is an area that is discussed within scholarly literature but "seldom discussed are issues on the basis of skin color" (Hall, 2005) within the African American community. Most recently there has been more literature on the idea, but there is still so much that has been left untouched. I am sure that this is due to the sensitive nature of the subject matter. Since skin color bias historically has roots within slavery (Hill, 2002; Russell et al., 1992) discussing it is not something that is always welcomed.

In 1946 Charles Parrish published an article entitled *Color Names and Color Notions* which described the shades of Black people. The names that emerged were, "Half-White, Yaller, High Yellow, Fair, Bright, Yellow, Light, Dirty Yellow, High Brown, Olive, Light Brown, Teasing Brown, Creole Brown, Medium Brown, Brown, Brownskin, Tan, Dark Brown, Chocolate brown, Dark, Black, Rusty Black, Ink Spot, Blue Black and Tar Baby" (p. 14). Each of these names encompasses the dynamic of colorism. Parrish placed into words the various names that Black people utilized to describe one another by shade.

This recognition of each other by skin tone is the impetus of colorism.

While most people use the term colorism, it can also be found in scholarly and unscholarly literature as; Color complex (Golden, 2004), Color struck (Golden, 2004; Hunter, 2005; Russell et al., 1992), Color consciousness (Glenn, 2009; Golden, 2004; Wilder & Cain, 2010), Color socialization (Wilder & Cain, 2010), Colorist ideology (Wilder & Cain, 2010), Colorist tragedy (Golden, 2004), Internalized skin tone bias (Wilder & Cain, 2010), Intragroup racism (Burton et al., 2010), Normative colorism (Wilder & Cain, 2010), Pigmentocracy (Golden, 2004), Racial stratification (Burton et al., 2010), Skin Color Bias (Glenn, 2009), Skin color socialization (Hunter, 2005; Wilder & Cain, 2010) and Skin tone stratification (Wilder & Cain, 2010). Each of these names will be used interchangeably throughout the remainder of this book with the understanding that they mean the same thing. I am certain that there are many other names by which this phenomenon is known; these are the descriptions that I found in the most prevalent works on the subject matter.

### Early Stages of Colorism

Skin tone variances began because of miscegenation, which is the mixing of races (Russell et al., 1992). In alignment with the rapes that took place during the middle passage (Byfield, Denzer, & Morrison, 2010) masters of slaves victimized Black women by using them as their outlet for sexual pleasure (Hunter, 2005). As a result, many shades of Blackness were derived. This new hybrid breed of Black people were considered *mulatto's,* meaning child of Black and white decent (Forbes, 1993). Many people believe that the master and his family treated these children better because he was their father, thus these children are said to have had easier labor, many times resulting in housework over field work (Russell et al., 1992). This phenomenon helped to coin the term "field negro" and "house negro." Many Black people attribute this to root of colorism, and still make reference to it when talking about the concept.

This is documented in so many books and articles, that the information is overwhelming. There are few who believe that this account of history may not actually be true. During earlier years, Parrish (1946) argued that very dark or Black Negros were preferred to lighter shades. His view was supported by referencing the image of the 'Black Mammy.' He called attention to the tradition of advertisements that almost invariably depicted Negroes as dark or Black. It is not difficult for me to follow Parrish's thought process because understanding the complexity of slavery it is hard to imagine that any slave, especially one who was a lighter complexioned because their mother was a product of rape, was given preferential treatment. It would be more conceivable to think that they were out casted from the master's family because they were a constant reminder of the indiscretions that the husband had committed. Unfortunately, the [white] master narrative within the African American community states otherwise, thus it is the one that is most believed. Because the victimization of Black women being raped, over the years Black people became lighter. Once freed from slavery those who could pass did so.

### Passing

Passing for white meant that a person did not have to endure the belligerence of being a person of color during this era. It is noted that to keep the "asset" of lightness so that others could pass a blue vein society was formulated (Russell et al., 1992). There are many historians, which document the passing of white and the inner turmoil it caused the person who lived the life of passing. To know that one's total identity is based on false pretense generated by the desire to have privilege and access is, as one can imagine, a life filled with fear and unquestionable truths that can never be uncovered, yet if people had the ability to pass for white, they did.

A very dear friend of mine told me a story about her cousins, one male and two females, who could pass for white during the early 1900s. In order to completely be accepted however they had to move away from their southern home to a northern state and start over. Each sibling married and never publicly acknowledged each other when out because of the fear of someone making a connection of their past. One day the brother and his white wife had a child that came out very dark complexioned. The newborn child uncovered the man's dark secret, and because of it the man nearly lost his life, after the men of town beat him to what they thought was his death. Fortunately, the man survived but had to return back to the south for his safety. After hearing of this incident, the sisters quickly retreated to their southern home to get "fixed" to not be able to have children, all so that they could return back to their northern "white" lives. This story is one of many of these types of occurrences that happened during our history (Kawash, 1996). Unfortunately, this passing went on for decades along with the slow evolution of Black people's freedom from slavery. By the early 1900's with the early rise of the civil rights movement, colorism began to take on a new face.

### Too Light—Too Dark

During the civil rights era, what it meant to be Black evolved. Keith and Herring (1991) state "a surge of Black nationalism proclaimed that 'Black is beautiful,' and skin tone declined in importance as a basis of prestige within the Black community" (p. 761). Although true, the literature notes a very specific division deepening between variances of shades within the Black community. Lighter skinned people are said to have begun using the paper bag test which allowed or denied entry and acceptance into many social organizations, churches and schools (Golden, 2004; Russell et al., 1992). "People who submitted to the paper bag test would often literally have a brown paper bag held up close to their face, and if they were darker than the bag would not be admitted to parties, sororities, and even some churches" (Golden, 2004, p. 23). Colleges & universities and sororities & fraternities are noted in their literature as the main perpetuators of the paper bag test (Maddox, 2004; Russell et al., 1992). In reminiscing about his personal experience with this during his tenure at Yale during the 1960s, Gates Jr. (1996) notes that the paper bag test was put to a stop immediately at Yale but was replaced by an opposite measure whereby those who were deemed not Black enough were shunned. Being too light automatically placed you in this category.

This inner turmoil of being too much of one shade and not enough of one shade was divisive. It began to create a culture of what Cooper-Lewter (1999) describes as "soul drive-bys" (p. 30). A soul drive-by is characterized by Black people being divisive and hurtful to one another due to grief. In this instance grief for being too light or grief from being too dark caused animosity and turmoil within the Black community.

> People experiencing Black grief contemplate following suit rather than continuing to repress their gut desires. Self-hate (acceptance of the dominant culture's view of us) thus makes violent Black-on-Black drive-bys attractive. The fact that the dominant culture may secretly approve, makes the consequences of our self-murder less costly. (p. 31)

The divisiveness based on skin tone was not rooted in just being Black but rather who was closer to white and who was not and what that meant during this time. The esthetic theme 'Black is beautiful' most clearly came to mean that whiteness was an unacceptable skin color (Goering, as cited in Hill, 2002) and anyone who resembled white was not Black enough. In contrast, "whiteness became identified with all that is civilized, virtuous, and beautiful; Blackness, in opposition, with all that is lowly, sinful, and ugly" (Hill, 2002, p. 77). So during this time there were two very different experiences that could have been happening. There were two very different narratives being created. Ultimately the ideology of race created the social construct of soul drive-bys.

**Which Black Is Beautiful**

With this division emerged the idea of beauty and who is actually the most beautiful within the race. That is what colorism is truly about. Most people try not to simplify it to aesthetics but the catalyst for it is skin tone. With that comes, features, such as but not limited to, hair, nose and any other attributes that can be compared to the idea of standard [white] beauty. Because beauty is a word used to describe the prototypical woman, in contrast masculine describes the ideal male. Colorism is usually associated with women. Tate (2007) notes that "the influence of whiteness as a yardstick for beauty has a history which extends back to slavery" (p. 301), which is exactly when the phenomenon began.

Men are affected by colorism but in a different way. Writer Itabari Njeri writes a story in Essence magazine entitled "Who is Black," which tells a different story. "Jeffrey, who looked like singer Ricky Nelson wanted to be 'the baddest nigger on the block.' Jeffrey died young on the streets trying to prove that he was not the enemy" (as cited in Russell et al., 1992, p. 66). Jeffrey was too light, and therefore was not deemed as not being *Black enough*. This idea can be prevailing for some Black people who were not born with a darker hue. Hill (2002) offers that the differences in the sexes in colorism can be noted as *gendered colorism*. In current times men very simply describe this by saying someone is in their light skin feelings which is not deemed as a compliment.

With the idea of colorism being rooted in beauty, it is evident to see that the next step that people would discuss in our heteronormative society is marriage. Marriage is documented as one of the most common benchmarks by which to measure the advantages and disadvantages of being lighter or darker (Golden, 2004; Glenn, 2009; Hunter, 2005; Russell et al., 1992). Some authors factually note that a light person marrying a light person was the only way the marriage equation should work, while other authors write that a dark person and a light person should marry but never two light people and never two dark people (Glenn, 2009; Hunter, 2005; Russell et al., 1992). This method of mixing shades was to ensure that the "right" shade of a child would be produced. Even with people knowing that the shade of the parent alone does not determine the shade of the child, many people believed in the proper mixing of genes to form the perfect complexion. This is one of many contradictions found within colorism.

My personal experience has been the later of the two. In fact, when I was dating one of the initial questions that my friends would ask me was "what complexion is he?" Anytime I have dated a lighter complexion man I can vividly see the disappointment in some of their faces which was usually followed by jokes of how bright our children would be if we ever had any. Likewise, any man who has been darker complexion, especially those who would be classified as "very dark" have been accepted with ease, with a follow up conversation of how beautiful our children would be if we were to ever procreate. I tell this story not as a way to make this about me but to show how common the ideals and beliefs learned many years ago, whether true or not, have seeped into our psyches and have become a part of everyday conversations.

**Family**

Although there is a dearth of scholarly research on colorism, so far, the points which I have highlighted are what I have found to be the foundational tenants of the idea. Most authors who have written about this phenomenon, especially those that are most cited such as Glenn (2009), Golden (2004), Hunter (2005), and Russell et al. (1992) have all discussed colorism in different ways. Additionally, Wilder and Cain (2010) also noted these areas in their work. What they do, however, is take it a step further by exploring the influence that families have on the formation and perpetuation of the color complex.

In a collaborative study, they explored the color complex and its original formulation amongst family members, more specifically women. Through narrative inquiry they were able to more intimately connect the beginning as well as the continued cycle of the phenomenon. Although many of the responses captured during the focus groups were atypical and biased in nature, they did come to a conclusion that normative colorism begins with the family. This is an important finding, because it gives insight into one of the ways that colorism still exists today.

Wilder and Cain (2010) were also successful at defining key moments, in the development of colorism, which are reaffirming and transformative. Reaffirming are the times in women's lives where ideals and beliefs they hold true are validated. Transformative are the times in their lives that are most critical and helped to form who they are. Both aid in the complex cycle in the lives of women of color.

Golden (2004) titled her book *Don't Play in the Sun* to mimic the words she often heard from her own mother in an effort to shield her from the complexities of colorism. Her accounts of her formative years and her mother and father's influence on her belief in her shade were shown on every page of her work. Even in growing older she never got away from what she heard and felt as a child. In one instance she talked about her son and his friends and their disdained emotions on dating darker complexioned girls. Even as a mother of an adult child, the very mention of her son and his friends having the conversation about dark skinned girls and light skinned girls took Golden back to earlier days in her life where colorism ruled her complete identity. She told her son, "Dark-skinned Black girls better have attitude. That's the only thing that saves them in a world that pretends they're not there or tries to erase them" (p. 58). This account, and many others in her well-chronicled book, is just one example which validates the work done by Wilder and Cain (2010). Golden even wrote, "it is within our families that we learn to support, encourage, believe in, or deny the color complex" (Golden, 2004, p. 39). I agree with them all.

While Burton et al. (2010) also discusses the ideology of colorism and the family influence they do so with the intention that it is one of the many tenants of critical race theory, which states "everyone within racialized social systems may contribute to the reproduction of these systems through social practices" (p. 442). Their belief is that colorism is a part of the overall infrastructure of racism; therefore, they examine it in conjunction with critical race theory as opposed to a separate entity. Because family is a strong part of who we become, learning about colorism negatively within the family infrastructure can be dangerous.

You probably have noticed that I have delegated colorism to light and dark. This is because research has shown that women of hues in between those shades are protected by the *intra* turmoil of colorism. In most studies a browner hue is desired as the most common shade (Hill, 2002; Hunter, 2005; Wilder & Cain, 2010). I must admit as a child this was the complexion I desired to be as well. It just seemed "safe." Golden (2004) asserts that women who are either very dark or very light are the ones who are tormented by the color complex.

Although Golden's work is autobiographical, with no reference to any scholarly literature, it has been one of the most quoted works within the body of work on colorism. This is because her story confirms the master narrative that suggests that dark is bad, and light is good. It tells a familiar story. There within lies the complexity of the issue. Concurrently, in their conclusion Wilder and Cain (2010) acknowledge that many girls did not share in the sentiments that light was better, and dark was bad, but yet they still chose to highlight those stories that reaffirm that stereotype. Although much more research intensive, Russell et al. (1992) also makes several claims concerning colorism and the preference for light over dark that, at times, are not supported with documentation but often taken for face value. Here again the master narrative is taken for the absolute truth. Truths without questions are always dangerous.

## Conclusion

Writing about a subject in a way that is familiar is more easily accepted because it reaffirms what people believe. I am a light skinned Black woman. In every instance I have been in, I have always been classified as that. Because of this I have found it difficult to read academic work that makes definitive claims about what it means to be light based on what is familiar but may not have been rooted in research. In writing this I recognize the extreme complex notion of my social class in challenging who gets heard especially as I stand as a Black Feminist. Even being true I have issues with scholarly text that reaffirm one "truth." I am a work in progress. If I believed everything that I read then I am supposed to be living in a better world than those around me who do not share my same hue simply because I am lighter complexion. This has not been my experience therefore it is not my reality. Concurrently, I know many others who would share this same belief. Thankfully I have been given the platform to take my experiences and thread them interchangeably using scholarly language to create a counter narrative to the current master narrative.

This counter narrative questions the said norms with the full intent to explore them from a different perspective. Colorism is a topic that deserves this type of attention because it is an issue that is talked about in everyday conversations. I am not refuting any work that has been done. I am simply adding to the conversation.

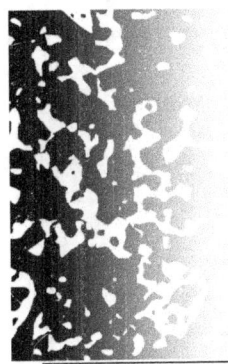

CHAPTER THREE

# Skin Tone and Attitude: Color Stratification Amongst Black Actresses

*She is desired and yet she is disliked. What she has others want, but she is not even sure that she wants what she has herself. She is told what she is and many times in her silence she accepts it. Images are being portrayed of her being one way, but what if she is not that way. She is told that she hurts others and that she discriminates against people who share her same race. Her skin apparently causes hurt and for that again she is silenced. Men want her but this doesn't give her worth. She wants to feel respected. She is isolated by the dominant race for being Black and then she is isolated by the Black race for being too light. Where does she fit in? Does anyone even care? She is discussed but the way in which she is always says the same thing, and it is never what she wants to hear. She is me and while I cannot speak for every light skinned Black woman I am frustrated as to how we have been spoken for through the years. Furthermore, I am perplexed that this voice is one that others desire.*

## Introduction

No matter where I go or who I perceive myself to be, the American society will always see me as a Black woman. Social identifiers are placed on us from the time we are born to help us distinguish one from another. Race and gender are two of the most visible and therefore dominant social identifiers that are with us from birth. What is next to come, religion, social class, nationality, and physical and mental ability are also quickly attached to our lives. Andersen and Collins (1998) state it this way, "Race is far from being the only significant marker of group difference-class, gender, sexuality, religion, and citizenship status all matter greatly in the United States" (as cited in Collins, 2000, p. 23). The ways in which we live, breath and move are influenced by the multiple ways we self-identify and moreover, are identified by others. "We are each born into a specific set of *social identities* . . . . . . . and these social identities predispose us to unequal *roles* in the dynamic system of oppression" (Harro, 2000, p. 15). Not every identity that we possess is oppressive, but every identity that we possess does have some type of social capital or lack thereof.

Some social values are considered to be negative, while others are considered to be positive. Two that I possess and embrace are being Black and being a woman; everything I see and feel is experienced existentially through this lens on life. Being a Black woman is a point of pride and strength for me and although I cannot speak for every Black woman, I concur with the sentiments of Patricia Hill Collins who said, "although racial segregation is now organized differently than in prior eras, being Black and female in the United States continues to expose

African-American women to certain common experiences" (Collins, 2000, p. 23). Black women themselves can only truly understand these experiences.

Arguably, even with our shared experiences there are numerous possible configurations of our identities and multiple ways in which what it means to be Black and concurrently a woman is shaped and reshaped many times, many ways and by many different forces. One area where this is most evident is how Black women have been situated within popular culture. Popular culture is the collection of ideas, beliefs and attitudes that are created and reproduced by mass media. In order for popular culture to be as its first word suggests, popular, there must be shared "buy- in" to the ideas and images that are being portrayed (Ashby, 2006; Storey, 2006). Popular culture and media help to perpetuate stereotypes which promote the idea that images that are seen are true representations of reality (West, 1995).

In this chapter I discuss the influence that media and popular culture have on the overall perception of Black women. I review the roles that Black women have been traditionally casted in as well as the roles that have been celebrated by the movie academy over the years. I specifically discuss the skin tone that is associated with each stereotypical role. I move my focus to the character that light skinned Black actresses have been portrayed in movies. Black Feminist Thought (BFT) is the theory which guides me through this process. It assumes that:

1. Racism, sexism, and classism are interlocking systems of oppressions
2. We must maintain a humanist vision that will not accept any amount of human expression.
3. We must define ourselves and give voice to the everyday Black woman and everyday experiences.
4. We must operate from the standpoint that Black women are unique and our experienc-

es are unique. (Collins, as cited in Woodard & Mastin, 2005 p. 267)

Utilizing this theory helps me to maintain the overall thread of the social construction of race in America.

**Film Industry**

According to Forbes the Film industry, which includes the Box office and Home/Mobile entertainment grossed 101 billion dollars in 2019. With this astronomical amount of money made, one must pause to think about how many people watched movies last year alone. Because of this, it is impossible to ignore the influence that media have on our lives. Historically films on the big screen have been used to depict fairy tale ideas of what life should be like. Most often people want to actualize these dreams as reality. However,

> When most Black people in the United States first had the opportunity to look at film and television, they did so fully aware that mass media was a system of knowledge and power reproducing and maintaining white supremacy. (hooks, 2003, p. 95)

The time that we spend investing our energy in movie images is the time that we spend being shaped and reshaping images of our self and others. Considering that "almost every time we have a choice about what to do with our lives, we choose to stare into a screen" (Dill, 2009, p. 39), this idea is daunting. Just as much as anything else films have shaped the way in which society views Black women.

There is an entire industry dedicated to heightening the received idea of women of color. Ladson-Billings (2009b) states, "stereotypes of Black women as Mammies, Sapphires, and Jezebels originated in American slavery and continue in the postmodern era" (p. 88). These roles have shaped the collective identity of Black women for years. "Portraying African-American women as stereotypical mammies, matriarchs, welfare recipients, and hot mommas helps justify U.S. Black women's oppression. Challenging these controlling images has long been a core theme in Black feminist thought" (Collins, 2000, p. 69).

## Mammy, Sapphire, and Jezebel

### Mammy

Traditionally the character of a mammy has been used as a controlling figure to depict Black women. It is one of the most pervasive images which originated during slavery (West, 1995). Through the years the mammy has been portrayed as a large, dark skinned Black woman whose sole purpose in life was to take care of her master's needs. Although she experienced comforts of living in the master's house, she was always on duty and expected to tend to the wishes of the first family (White, 1999). Because the mammy was usually considerably overweight, she usually draped herself in clothes large enough to cover a room (Harris, 1982; West, 1995). The mammy image depicted strength, loyalty, and tradition according to the [white] master narrative. Almost always this character is depicted as a dark-skinned woman.

In 1939 Hattie McDaniel made history by being the first Black woman to receive an academy award for best supporting actress for her role as mammy in *Gone with the Wind*. Her role reinforced the stereotype of Black women as submissive servants. On the night of winning her award Ms. McDaniel was the only Black person present who was not a maid or an attendant. The National Association for the Advancement of Colored People (NAACP) was displeased with the movie and the role that she played. They were not the only ones. Many other Black people were upset of her portrayal in the film, which depicted a role from which Black women as a whole were trying to distance themselves.

Hattie McDaniel's stereotypical role illuminates how forms of racism are enacted in society through film. In media Black women are not the controllers of our images, therefore are unable to decide what pictures represent who we are. Mammy was one of the first controlling images applied to Black women's identity (Collins, 2000) and has been used as the benchmark by which to describe and characterize strength of a Black woman. The image of mammy has been accepted by white mainstream America as a "symbol of patriarchal tradition" (White, 1999, p. 58) so much so that through the years three of the nine Black actresses who won academy awards did so for playing this role. After Hattie McDaniel there was Whoopi Goldberg for her role as a modern-day mammy in *Ghost* in 1990 and Octavia Spencer for her role in *The Help* in 2009. "The mammy image has appeared to impact the psychological functioning of Black women" (West, 1995). Although accepted by white mainstream America overall the image of mammy is not something that has been embraced by the Black community.

## Sapphire

The next stereotypical role, the sapphire, also known as the "angry Black woman" and/or the super-bitch (Bogle, 2001; Collins, 2005; Ladson-Billings, 2009b; West, 1995) originated from a character on the radio show Amos 'n Andy. Sapphire Stevens frequently berated her husband on the program. Women in these roles are known to be sassy, rude, arrogant, and disruptive to the family structure. Although not being the first role that Black women were recognized for, this show was popular during the time that *Gone With the Wind* first premiered, which means that this role has been around just as long as the mammy role. The longevity of both is alarming.

In 2006 Jennifer Hudson won an academy award

# Skin Tone and Attitude: Color Stratification

for her character as Effie Melody in *Dream Girls*. A few years later, in 2008 Monique Imes-James also won an academy award for her role as Mary in *Precious*. Followed by Viola Davis who won for her role as Rose Maxon in Fences in 2016. Each woman can be categorized as sapphires. The complexion of a woman playing a sapphire is typically brown skinned. Although this role is mainly associated with brown skinned Black women, the sassiness that is associated with being a sapphire has almost become synonymous with being a Black woman. As if to say if you are Black and you have some type of attitude then you must be angry.

**Jezebel**

The final stereotypical role that Black women have been casted in is the role of a jezebel. A jezebel is considered to be the antithesis of the mammy character. Whereas the mammy is considered to be undesirable the jezebel is the complete opposite. The name has historical roots to an evil queen in the bible. She is known as a very promiscuous woman who uses sex to gain what she wants. Much like the other stereotypical characters this role can be tricky because it leads to further discussion about double standards between men and women and Black and white.

The image of the jezebel has been in movies for almost a century now. The first woman to play this role was Nina Mae McKinney in the film *Hallelujah* in 1929. In this role she was described as a sexy, seductive chic (Howard, 1996). When actresses such as herself and Lena Horne "appeared in mainstream cinema most white viewers were not aware that they were looking at Black females unless the film was specifically coded as being all Blacks" (hooks, 2003, p. 97). Because *Hallelujah* was an all-Black cast it was easy to see that McKinney was Black, as such she was casted as a jezebel.

The role of jezebel reinforces the stereotype of the "tragic mulatto whom historically have been portrayed as a sexually attractive, light skinned woman of African American heritage who could pass for white" (Pilgrim, as cited in Kretsedemas, 2010, p. 152). This character is not the whole of who she is, but rather she exists in relationship to another; a man.

> Thus humanity is male and man defines woman not in herself but as relative to him; she is not regarded as an autonomous being ... For him she is sex- absolute sex, no less. She is defined and differentiated with reference to man and not he with reference to her; she is the incidental, the inessential as opposed to the essential. He is the Subject, he is the Absolute—she is the other. (Hesse-Biber, 2007, p. 1)

Women in general are seen in this way in movies and in life, but the emphasis is that much more when you are a Black woman, especially one with lighter skin. So was the case with Halle Berry in *Monster's Ball*.

In 2001, Halle Berry made history by becoming the first Black woman to receive and Academy Award for best leading actress. Her character Leticia Musgrove was married to a Black man on death row. After the death of her husband Leticia became the object of affection of a white man named Hank Grotowski played by Billy Bob Thornton. A scene in the movie where Hank bent Leticia over a chair and began to penetrate her is what many believe won Berry the award. Berry's character portrayed the often duplicated image of a Black woman as a jezebel and for this she was awarded. "As cathartic as the narrative renders it, their sexual relationship still stands out as a contrived plot point and one of the most implausible aspects of *Monster's Ball*" (Mask, 2009, p. 230). The movies runtime is one hundred eleven minutes, but two minutes is all that most people remember or even care to talk about.

Don't believe me? Ask any person who watched the movie and what they remember about it. This scene caused much conversation among critics and members of the African American community. Although Black women's roles in film can be traced back to as early as the 1900s, no Black woman had ever received an Oscar for best actress until Berry did so. "*Monster's Ball* reveals the relationship between race, gender, and class" (Mask, 2009, p. 230). There is no coincidence that a sexually explosive scene which depicted Berry as an over sexed woman was attached to this award.

Unsurprisingly Denzel Washington received his first Oscar for best actor the same year Halle Berry did for his role as a crooked, dope dealing, killer cop in *Training Day*. Although he played many other roles prior to and after this one he never received another Oscar for leading actor, which is surprising to many especially since he had a groundbreaking performance in the movie *Malcolm X* where he played the civil rights activist himself.

Of all the roles that Berry played before this movie and the many roles she has played thereafter none have ever been talked about the way this one was. To date, Berry's role in *Monster's Ball* has been her most notable role.

## Trinary Thinking

Although there are multiple and competing ways of being a Black woman Hollywood has portrayed, casted and celebrated Black women in the three specific roles discussed in the previous section. Mammy, Sapphire and Jezebel are the images of who we are on the big screen (Bogle, 2001, 2007; Collins, 2005; Ladson-Billings, 2009b). Actresses in movies are used as an avenue to objectify Black women. In these roles they are placed into categories and it is in these three categories that have been accepted by mainstream America. Black Feminist Theory would question this given voice. Also, It would debunk the binary thinking, in this case I would call it "trinary" thinking which causes you to look at people or ideas in terms of either or, Harris (1982) contends that "the Black American Woman has had to admit that while nobody knew the troubles she saw, everybody, his brother, and his dog, felt qualified to explain her, even to herself" (p. 4). The image that has been portrayed in film is not a clear representation of who *we* are.

Black Feminist Thought petitions for voices of women of color collectively, especially those who may otherwise go unheard. It contends "that there can be no separation of ideas from experience and that Black feminism is not a set of abstract principles, but it is a set of ideas that come directly from the historical and contemporary experience of Black women" (Woodard & Mastin, 2005, p. 268). These experiences should be in alignment with what is being portrayed in film, but they are not.

Because people of color in general are not the main players in Hollywood *we* do not have the opportunity to speak with a voice or voices, which could serve as a better representation of Black women. The images that the academy have accepted and celebrated as the "controlling images of Black womanhood" (Collins, as cited in M. Williams, 2006, p. 203) symbolize the voice that they have chosen for us. I must note that I chose the academy award as the point of reference for success because it is the oldest and perceived highest award that any actress or actor can receive. Because Black women are all interconnected, our past has a strong influence on our present, which has an undeniable amount of authority on our future which is what I saw in examining these roles. The same characters that were portrayed in the early 1900s are the same characters that are portrayed today. This is evidenced in the first Oscar given to Hattie McDaniel and the most recent Oscar given to Ariana DeBose. The characters that Black women have been recognized for by the organization further illustrates the complexity of race, sexuality and the influence that imagery has on the collective identity of Black women.

## Stereotypes and Reality

Although my book is autobiographical in nature I felt it important to discuss the presence of Black women in movies for two reasons. First, Black women do not exist in isolation of each other and secondly, the stereotypes that are noted in film are the ones that are believed about women according to their shades. Each character that Black women have been known for over the years has and continues to have persons casted into the roles based on skin tone. Mammies have been darker complexion, sapphires have been brown to dark complexion and jezebels have been light complexion (Bogle, 2001; Collins, 2000). No complexion means more than the other especially in the context of the three stereotypes, yet the image of light skin is the one that is adorned.

If movies were just forms of entertainment this may not be such a big deal. Unfortunately, this is not the case. "From an evolutionary or biological perspective we are supposed to believe what we see, not doubt it" (Dill, 2009, p. 150). Most often what people see serves as actual reality for them thus seeing Black women cast typed and celebrated for these stereotypical roles is damaging to say the least. Movies influence our psyche and "visual imagery plays an important role in socialization, specifically in how we extract and apply meaning from everyday experience, and therefore in how we construct social realities" (Dill, 2009, p. 96). These realities guide our consciousness and become the blueprint by which we live our lives.

There are many stereotypes beyond the ones that are depicted in movies that are associated with skin tone, but the ones from movies are the ones that are most discussed, remembered and enacted in social conversations. Former first lady Michelle Obama has been publicly criticized by the media for years for being "too" strong. During her term she was forced to defend herself and was told who she was. Without saying it she was portrayed as the "angry Black woman" the sapphire. In fact, some public figures such as the late Rush Limbaugh and Jody Kantor have gone as far as saying she is such. This image of her being an angry Black woman was enacted in film many years before she was born, but because she is a brown skinned Black woman this stereotype has been associated with her life.

Beyoncé, on the other hand, has not been portrayed as an "angry Black woman" or a mammy, but rather a sex symbol, something to be desired. Her imagery was created on the big screen many years ago and she enacts it every time she performs. Although her image is the stereotypical jezebel which is associated with being a light skinned woman, it is not something that she ever has to defend. This is because to be desired by a man is to be validated for, he is supposed to be the gauge by which a woman's worth is confirmed. While the imagery of a jezebel is fictitious, it becomes real and easy to accept in true life because of its presence on the big screen.

### Light Skinned Objects

Contrary to popular belief, being light is not always what it is imagined to be. M. Williams (2009) had this to say about Lena Horne, a famous light skinned Black actress whose career began as early as 1939.

> Although Horne's skin tone and Anglicized features allowed for her success as Hollywood film star and glamour girl, the singer/actresses' skin color and physiognomy created issues for Horne among other African Americans. During her childhood, peers teased Horne regarding her skin color; at this young age Horne realized that, in the minds of some African Americans, "light color is far from being a status symbol." (p. 4)

There is a constant portrayal of beauty, sexuality and in many cases a snobbish or stuck up attitude that is associated with having lighter skin (Golden, 2004; Hunter, 2005). Historically light skinned women have been casted into jezebel roles. In turn they were usually seen as sex symbols or something to be desired. This symbol helped to further inscribe the collective identity of light skinned Black women as objects. Certainly it would be presumptions to assume that all light skinned women are jezebels, or brown skinned women are sapphires or dark-skinned women are mammies, but these are the images that have been portrayed over the years. Black actresses have won Oscars for roles that depicted them as "isolated African American characters as beholden to beneficence of white philanthropy, or at least, humbled by the moral rectitude of white paternalism" (Mask, 2009). These roles and images give people the model by which to receive others.

## My Fantasy and Reality

One of the six Black women who won the academy award, Whoopi Goldberg (1991) graciously thanked the audience on the night she won. She said, *"Ever since I was a little kid I wanted to do this. You don't know … …. I want to thank everybody who makes movies. I come from New York as a little kid I lived in the projects and you're the people I watched."* What she saw on the big screen became her reality. Much like Whoopi I too watched movies as a young child and was heavily influenced by what I saw. This could not have been truer then when I was a young girl watching *School Daze* by Spike Lee for the very first time.

## School Daze

In 1989 Spike Lee made a film entitled *School Daze*, which depicted the lives of students at a Historically Black College. Watching this movie for the very first time truly changed my life. I was too young to understand how much so, or what he was really trying to say in his movie, but I knew I was forever changed. The movies main character, Half Pint, played by Spike Lee, was on a mission to become a member of a fraternity called Gamma Phi Gamma. Through his glorified pledging process Half Pint became increasingly popular and was able to cross paths with members of the sister sorority the Gama Rays also known as the Wannabe's. The foes of these women were part of an unofficial organization called the Jigaboos. In the film the Wannabees were the light skinned girls, who wore contacts to lighten their eyes and were considered to have "good hair" which is very significant to the plot. The Jigaboos were darker skinned girls with "kinky hair" who were proud of their African heritage. For the purpose of the storyline, they were portrayed to be less attractive although in reality they were very gorgeous women.

As I later learned, each organization, including the fraternity that Half Pint was trying to join, was supposed to be a depiction of three Black Greek letter organizations that actually exist. The Gamma Rays were supposed to represent Alpha Kappa Alpha Sorority, Inc. (AKA). The group of women who were organized but were not considered a sorority were supposed to represent Delta Sigma Theta Sorority, Inc. (DST). The fraternity that Half Pint was trying to join was supposed represent Alpha Phi Alpha, Fraternity, Inc. (A-Phi-A; Lee & Jones, 1988). Dissecting *School Daze* to find traces of colorism is not necessary because they are obvious.

No scene in *School Daze* showed that more than one that took place in the beauty salon. It was there here that the rising tension between the two sororities erupted in an argument where slurs such as "Pickanniny, Barbie Doll, High Yellow Heffa, Tar Baby, Wanna- be-White, Jigaboo" were exchanged. As they sang "go on and swear; see if I care; good and bad hair" the two groups battled out their differences. The song also repeatedly said "you're just a jigaboo trying to find something to do; well, you're a wannabe, wannabe better than me." As a child, I sang along with the songs and was conflicted as to which sorority I fit with. Ascetically I knew that

# Skin Tone and Attitude: Color Stratification

I looked like the Gamma Rays (minus the hair) but based on the factor of being down to earth I thought I was a part of the other group. Why is this important? Again, what we see on the big screen becomes our reality. Spike Lee made it a strong part of his script to pit the women against each other. If you were watching it, you felt that you had to choose a side. Even as a young child I felt that pressure. I felt I had to be a part of either of the sororities. It never crossed my mind that I could be both or better yet neither. I felt that I had to choose. The movie also discussed class stratification as well as the underground process of pledging, which some say resemble the process of slavery.

As a young girl I noticed that Jane Toussaint played by Tisha Campbell was "friendly" with the men. In one of the final scenes of the movie she was prompted by her boyfriend Julian to sleep with Half Pint and with little reservation she did it. Again, I was too young to truly conceptualize what happened in that scene, but I knew that I did not want to be a wannabe because of that. Unfortunately, all my friends thought that is who I should be because of my skin tone.

Almost in the same way that an artist draws a caricature that calls attention to one's biggest or most distinct feature, Spike Lee used this movie to call attention to the nuisances of skin tone stratification. Lee is considered to be a controversial screenwriter, director and producer because of the type of messages that he depicts. *School Daze* was greeted with mixed reviews due to its sensitive nature.

Although very stereotypical the characters that Spike Lee portrayed are in alignment with those that are portrayed in all movies, which cast Black women. As discussed with each role comes a shade or complexion that is associated with the character. Over the years light-skinned women have been portrayed as the ones to be and for those who desire this perhaps that is something to be thrilled about, but what happens if that is not your desire? What happens if that is what you think people see when they see you?

I was heavily influenced by what I saw in *School Daze*. Once I learned that the "Wannabes" were emulating women of Alpha Kappa Alpha I did not want to be a part of that group at all. Ironically (or not) I ended up joining this very sorority. I'll talk more about this in my next chapter. Even as I type this I had to pause and think about just how much we are influenced in our formative years. Although *School Daze* reproduced stereotypical images it was made to speak to the consciousness of Black people. Spike Lee was critiquing the ways in which Black people have internalized skin tone stratification. Not many movies do this. I have young daughters and years later after Lee's movie this conversation is still very relevant. I am very troubled by the images that they are looking at now which are supposed to reflect who they are to become when they are adults. Even cartoons and kid shows have traces of *isms* in them.

## Conclusion

The same images of Black women have been depicted for over a century. These images have become a part of our psyche. "When people imagine a picture, they come to believe that they have actually seen that picture more often. . . . . . . if this occurs, people are providing their own imagined confirmation of their previously established stereotypes" (Dill, 2009, p. 97). Through the years Hollywood has enacted color stratification of Black women right before our very eyes. The dominance of race and racism are so deeply rooted in who have become that even with the constant bombarding of visual imagery it is difficult to see. The roles that Black women have been casted in over the years do nothing to resolve our already wounded souls. Each stereotypical role is associated with a complexion. For the mammy role there is the darker skinned woman, for the sapphire there is a brown skinned woman and for the jezebel there is a light skinned woman. One role is no better than the other, but there is a misperception that being light skinned is the role that you want to have.

When people see these images they believe they are what they are supposed to believe about Black women. Seeing a woman who aesthetically resembles who I am and knowing that she is being portrayed as jezebel or something to be desired does not make me proud. In fact it makes me feel the complete opposite. When I walk into a room of people, especially rooms that are filled with men, in many people's mind I assume the role of what they have seen in movies. I am mortified by this thought. Unfortunately, my fears have been validated over the years with the comments and unwanted advances made by men. Am I really supposed to be excited because I am the object of someone's desire?

In this chapter I examined the three roles that African American women have been casted in over the years. I focused my work with one of the roles, the jezebel, in an attempt to illustrate how light skinned African American women have been portrayed over time. Understanding that fantasy becomes reality seeing women in these roles has constructed the idea of what it means to be a light skinned Black woman according to popular culture.

My concern continues to be how all this shapes the identities of those who watch the films and how they later respond to what they have seen on the big screen. From watching films, we form our social identities, which inform us on how we should exist, and how we should perceive others existence in this world. The next chapter will discuss my personal experiences of being a light skinned Black woman during various time periods in my life.

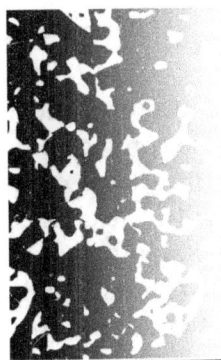

CHAPTER FOUR

# Tales of a Melantated Sistah: Journaling through Colorism

## Introduction

The wound of race and racism in America has become such a deep part of who we are as a country that most people accept it as "just is." Much like an actual scar that needs time to heal, so is the case with racism. People are hurt by it and as the old saying goes hurt people hurt other people. In the presence of this pain, it is easy for people to develop a sense of hopelessness. In 2001, West affirmed that "Black existential angst derives from the lived experience of ontological wounds and emotional scars inflicted by white supremacist beliefs and images permeating U.S. society and culture" (p. 27). Here we are 22 years later, and this same sentiment still holds true.

From racism stems other forms of oppressions that can be internalized and enacted. This is especially true, within communities of color. As you have read throughout this book, colorism is one of these forms. Because we are all a part of the same

social order having shared skin and even gender can cause one group of people to be connected in interlocking oppressions. Within this shared community, uncensored conversations often take place in what is considered a safe space. Because I am so intrinsically connected to Black people, especially Black women, I'm able to be involved in these types of conversations.

In the scope of this book, I have discussed race, racism, and colorism. My personal wounds from the three lead me to this chapter through my act of self-care, journaling. Writing down some of my most memorable experiences through the years and placing these stories in my work has given me the chance, as Grason (2005) says, to "jump off a few cliffs and reveal myself to another human being" (p. xii). Because of this leap I have found this chapter to be most difficult to construct. I found myself wanting to rewrite some of the stories because I was angry, sad, or frustrated, but in the true nature of being authentic, I left them as is.

In my fullness I share some moments that I haven't talked about in years; moments that I realized throughout this process I have never truly dealt with myself. This is where my herstory meets my educational knowledge and my feelings meet my reality. This process has unraveled me in ways that quite honestly, I have not always welcomed. But as you might remember from a previous chapter, my greatest desire is to be authentic with my work and experiences, which is why I share this with you. In this chapter I am reminded that the personal is always political.

At the beginning of my book, I named five areas which the literature states as being influenced by having lighter skin. These areas are spouses, children, employment, social organizations, and education. Overall, the literature suggests that having Black skin that is lighter will give you a better quality of life. After reading through my narratives, I found that some of these themes emerged, but more commonly more robust categories were formulated.

I strongly believe that this variance in what I read and what I actually experienced and heard is common. Most of the other studies on colorism have been quantitative.

The following list outlines the common themes:

1. Family
2. Children
3. Church
4. Social Organizations & Status
5. Men
6. Popular Culture & Self Perception
7. Self- Actualization

The remainder of this chapter will discuss these areas through the use of narratives.

## Family

Most people learn about colorism through the socialization of their family (Wilder & Cain, 2010). I am no different. As a child most of my nicknames originated because of my complexion. My mom called me a version of Winnie the Pooh because I was a "yellow" kid. Other names I was called by others were tweety bird (I actually embraced this name), Big Bird, Hiawatha, Pac Girl, the Black Annie, and my all-time disliked one, a Yellow Banana. I knew early on that my complexion gave me a lot of attention; the type of attention that I did not like. I wanted to be brown so bad and only wished that I could be my mother's complexion. I honestly felt her brown skin saved her from ridicule. I recognized as a child that being any darker than her would not have shielded me from name calling because I too heard the names that people with a darker hue were being called. I must admit that at times I may have felt vindicated because of the way that some of them tormented me. I had a hard time embracing the nicknames because I felt they were given to me because of something that I could not control, my complexion.

Now having children of my own who are different shades I can see the complexity of colorism seeping through the thoughts spoken and unspoken from our family, village and even strangers. My desire to be my mother's complexion came through the birth of my first daughter. If I thought being lighter was a point of contention for some people, I never considered how being lighter and birthing a brown skinned daughter would refocus my understanding. I feel that she may stand in the crossroads of my trauma because she and I have different hues. This totally shifts my mindset on brown skin people being shielded from the nuances of colorism. My husband and I have both had to gently correct family members on their language as it pertains to our daughter. As you can imagine we are very intentional about this. Even still my oldest daughter has already developed a dominant understanding on complexion as she colors her artwork from school with light skin and yellow hair.

I wish I could say that I did not think that colorism was learned in my family, aside from the nicknames that I was called as a child but that simply is not the case. One day while having a conversation with an elder in my family I listened intently to the ways in which she described her complexion as well as the complexion of others in my family. The idea of all of us being paper bag safe (her words not mine) pierced my spirit. Her thoughts on the preference of the skin tone of her own partners reaffirmed all that I had read in my research but again I question some of those things now. What is still apparent to me however is that colorist ideologies are real, and they are learned.

I think all of this is magnified in families by the many messages that are spoken to children on a daily basis. When I was a child, they did not make dolls in the many shades that I now see for my own children. My favorite doll growing up was a white cabbage patch named Jolene. Oh, how I loved her so. There were Black versions of her, but I did not want them because I did not think they looked like me. Instead, I rubbed my doll in the dirt often to make her darker. Even then I understood the importance of having something or someone that I could connect to. Many children don't have this same capacity to do this. They accept what they see with what they hear and unfortunately most of these messages are indoctrinated in the false belief of white superiority. In turn some brown families turn around and begin to ingrain the trauma from these thoughts into the next generation. You would think that as far as we've come as a people that we would be keenly aware of how dangerous this is but as I often tell my students, hegemony is a helluva drug.

Within the past couple of years, I had a family member send me a post on social media which magnified the idea of authentic Blackness being strongly attributed to being a darker hue. It made me think more about how we normalize shades and complexions further in families and what type of space this takes up generationally. Perhaps this lends to a different conversation on colorism, the one that is most often had, but it still aligns with this idea of being taught in families. I didn't agree with her post. I also did not tell her that I I did not agree with it. I wasn't prepared to have that conversation because as brave as I am, I'm still finding my voice as it relates to this topic. In life I believe we can always be both and at the same time. Throughout our childhood we are always getting message about our adult selves. It would make sense then for colorism to show up adulthood.

### Why Would I Do This to My Kids?

Of all the things that baffle me about colorism, it is this belief that having light skin will give you a better chance at a relationship and children. The next journal entry took place after talking with a former student on campus who organized a program about this very topic.

I was so glad that I ran into Crystal today. I wasn't able to attend the session that her organization put on concerning colorism so I couldn't wait to speak with her. Actually, I didn't know she was the president of the group: I just knew she was active with the group, so when I got the details from her, they were intricate indeed. When I asked her how the program went, she floored me with all the details.

First, she told me that the students did an exercise where they had to break off into groups based on shade. She shared that although this was meant to simply be an icebreaker things quickly got interesting as people were "denied" access to a group while others were sent to another group because they did not fit in where they were standing. She told me that this happened with all the groups. Although she never said which groups they had she did say it was three which led me to believe that they were light brown, medium brown and dark brown. I did not ask her, but I was very curious to know which group had the most issues in terms of turning people away. She later told me that the discussions they had were very heated and that it was very divided by complexions of people. Crystal considers herself to be light skin. I'm sure most would agree with her. She said that one of the biggest arguments that she had was "why would I want to have a child. Why would I want them to experience this"? She said that she would not want to give her child her skin because she wouldn't want her to go through what she had gone through.

Unfortunately, I knew what she meant. I too have had those same thoughts in the past. The teasing, the picking, the idea that people think you believe you are better than them because you are light skinned can be hard to bear. Although I wanted to ask her more, I knew exactly what she was saying. It was the same belief that always led me to believe that I would marry and procreate with a man of darker complexion to simply give my children a chance at peace beyond their skin tone. I moved past those thoughts, but listening to this young, yet mature college student, I knew that she had not, and wondered how many other college students felt the same way.

I once worked with a woman who was of darker hue who shared the same sentiments that Crystal did. I'll never forget the pain in her eyes as she looked at me and said, "I'll never have kids because I do not want to do THIS to my children." ... She was beautiful. She also was in a lot of pain. I could see the admiration in her eyes as she idolized my skin. I wanted to share with her that I understood yet I knew that moment was not about me and that most people who are of darker hue would not be able to understand for I have the very thing they believe they want, and I can understand why. Light is glorified because light is closer to white. I don't want it to be missed that I understand this. I also don't want it to be missed that when you are lighter complexioned and Black you are still Black.

To answer the question of why anyone would want to do this to their kids is complicated. My mature self says why not? I do I understand however that it took me many years to have this type of understanding and that not everyone is willing and or able to do the necessary work to get to this space. After revisiting these stories, I felt that same feeling as I did when I once journaled them and that is sad. Many years later I have been faced with more stories like this. Many years later I'm still at a loss as to what to say to people. My work has been done in silence but in person I am still the woman who sat in my professor's office with my colleagues and shrunk at the idea of telling a story about colorism that was different from the one that is most often told. Nonetheless here we are, and the next reflection is one that takes the most courage to share. As I began to do this work, I took some time to reflect on my pathway of becoming a member of the most prestigious organization in the Divine Nine.

### Not Wanting to Be an AKA

In my last chapter I began a discussion about the movie School Daze and the impact that it had on my childhood. Once I realized that the organizations in the movies were strongly mirroring real sororities, I knew which one that I did not want to join and that was Alpha Kappa Alpha, Sorority, Inc. (AKA) Spoiler alert, that is the very organization I joined.

The teenage years are so formative in a young person's life, especially with young ladies. It is here when the early division of spectator and participant truly begins. It is also here when girls are most self-conscious about their appearance and when they begin to divide based on whatever silly differences or similarities, they believe they have. So was the case in my middle school years. Because there is only one member of a Greek letter organizations in my family, I actually learned about sororities from my peers at school and School Daze. I constantly heard that I was going to be an AKA when I grew up. I was mortified by this thought because those were the women in the film who were conceited. Suddenly the characters in School Daze seemed so very real. Whereas I still never decided if I wanted to be a "Jiggaboo" or a "Wannabe" my position was chosen for me by my peers. I did not like that feeling nor did I embrace it.

Internally I was baffled by the thought that anyone would think I was stuck up or thought of myself as being better than them. I could only assume that is what they thought of me based on the film I watched. I lived in the same neighborhood they did. If that wasn't the case I felt that we at least went to the same school which meant that their neighborhoods looked like my own so how could they think this of me? My only comeback was "No way, I'm not going to be an AKA I'm going to be a Delta because they are down to earth and so am I." I had this position until I got to college and thought enough to actually research all the organizations. Turns out they were right. AKA was a better fit for me and not for the reasons I believe they felt which were being light skin, pretty and, or stuck up (all but one of these given attributes can be debatable) but rather because they stood for high scholastic achievement, unity, friendship, and service to all mankind, which was important to me. I thought long and hard about being a Delta. Everyone I knew growing up was one, and all my friends wanted to join them, but it just was not a good fit for me. If my only motivation was to prove everyone wrong I knew that was not enough for me. I found peace in knowing that the values I believed in so did the women of Alpha Kappa Alpha Sorority, Inc. I was also old enough to know that the stereotypes that I heard over the years simply were not true for either sorority. They both have wonderful and well-balanced women in their organizations.

It is my life practice to be open and honest when teaching and working with people. As such whenever I am facilitating any conversation that is directly or sometimes even loosely related to colorism I feel it very important to be upfront about my organization. More importantly I want to create an open space for what it may mean (if at all) to the people whom I am working with. Although I know, and most people do too, that the stereotypes about sororities are not true it is still a conversation that I have to have. Quite honestly the conversation makes me uncomfortable, but I know it is necessary. After teaching my first undergraduate class session on colorism I wrote:

I was so nervous today in front of the students. I really tried hard to distance myself from the subject matter and I knew they sensed it. Looking out at the class I could not help but feel that many of them were thinking "how can she tell us about this?" I made it a point to not pull out my laptop (which is pink and green) and made sure that I had nothing on my key ring which would give away my sorority. Normally I would not think that a student on this predominately white campus would pick up on these subtleties, but this class is different. This

class is filled with majority Black students, they would know. It is not that I am ashamed of being an AKA. In fact, the opposite is true. It's that me saying that I am one automatically validates some people's assumptions about the organization and perhaps about me. Of all the countless conversations and debates I had with people where I try to inform them that the stereotypes about AKA's are not real and that we don't take people based on skin tone it always ends in "look at you." Suddenly in that moment I'm deflated because my past five to ten minutes of words meant nothing. Especially the part of me saying "I have so many sorors who are not light skinned!" Also in that moment I feel that I sound like a white person who says "I have Black friends" so I stop. I don't know how to get past that.

After the session the professor on record gave me feedback on my teaching. He said I did a great job but I needed to open up a little more so they could connect with me. Even he sensed me trying to disconnect myself from the subject. I left from his feedback asking myself why do I do that? I tried the same thing in book seminar, and it didn't work then either. Why am I so afraid to make myself a part of the narrative?

Now some time later looking at this particular reflection I can answer the question clearly. I don't want to offend anyone with my truth. Although I know there are multiple and competing truths, I understand that the narrative that I offer could be contentious and potentially offensive to people of a darker hue. On the opposite side of that however I understand that there are girls and women with little girl memories inside of them of lighter hue who have probably suffered in silence for this same reason. And to know that all of this is systemic from racism gives me the courage and space to speak my truth. My Black truth. My absolute truth.

I'm grateful that I joined my sorority. I love the sisterhood and will constantly try to dispel the myth of a stuck-up Alpha Kappa Alpha woman. Additionally, I have the upmost respect for the women of

Delta Sigma Theta, Sorority, Inc. Even through the difficult conversations I will continue to educate those who care to listen. What frustrates me the most is I know I am so much more than a stereotype, but then again I feel that same way about being a Black woman in general, AKA aside. The fact that it is virtually impossible to escape conversations connected to colorism is exhausting. In regard to this even the Black church is not a safe space.

### Even Tanning Can't Take the Pain Away

Because I am self-proclaimed believer I always consider how what I learn in the classroom aligns with what I am learning at church. Over the years I have tried hard to keep the two as separate as possible because most times they do not align. This is especially true since my research is on race, racism and colorism. I truly believe that God does not see color. I never really heard anyone talk about their own issue with color stratification in a church setting until I attended a fellowship for women early one Saturday morning. This is why the next story intrigued me so much.

To fellowship with one's community of believers is to come together with like-minded spirits to talk about the goodness of our heavenly father and the life that lies there within. This particular Saturday was special because one of the high-ranking officials of the church had recently gotten married. His wife, Natalie, was being introduced into the church community. Natalie is absolutely beautiful, both inside and out. She has very light skin, keen features, sandy brown hair, light eyes and a slim waist. I find it important to note that her features of lightness are not what makes her beautiful; features completely opposite of what is listed would make her equally as beautiful, but rather her heart for God is what shines the most.

Natalie began to share her life, or her testimony as "church folk" call it with the ladies who were present. She grew up in a rural community in North

Carolina. She was a product of single parent home, where her mother and her grandmother raised her. She never knew her father growing up and expressed a void in her life because of that. As she continued to testify about her upbringing, she especially got sentimental when she began to talk about her skin tone. She told a story of a young child whom others teased because she was so light skinned. Because of this during the summer months she would stay outside for long periods of time to get darker. Unfortunately, her getting a tan only caused her to burn which in turn caused more ridicule, but now by her caregivers and even some of the same kids who teased her for being too light.

She went on to tell us that she never felt accepted because of this ridicule and how it prompted her to look for love in all the wrong places. She just never felt quite "Black enough" is how she put it. This caused a major void in her life. It was not until she found Christ did her desire to find acceptance become fulfilled. In this instance Natalie was able to do what most women aren't able to do. Her vulnerability resonated with me greatly and reaffirmed for me that I was not alone. I couldn't imagine that I'd hear about colorism again in the church until one day I did again.

It seemed like Natalie coming to the church brought out the color complex in a lot of us. It is usually not a conversation that is often had in that space especially when Black people are among mixed racial company, but healing takes place when and where it needs to. Albeit it true, I'd be lying if I said that it wasn't a big exhausting to hear the many conversations about colorism there as I go to church to escape the troubles of the world. I do understand however that being a part of a predominantly Black church that much of the issues that are relevant to me are also relevant to others. With that I make peace. I also understand that racism and colorism are in the very fabric of our being. Why would I think of church to be any different? At least at church I only had to listen. In other spaces I might have to actually engage in conversation with someone regarding colorism and that is never conversation that I ever really want to have.

## Self-Actualization—Proving My Blackness

Most people who know me fairly well know that I have a strong attachment to colorism; so although I may not always want to talk about it, the conversation seems to find me. One day in talking with a dear friend I was asked if I felt that I had to defend my Blackness to others. Without hesitation I answered yes, depending on where I am or who I am with. One thing is for sure however is that I never have to convince white people that I am Black which further frustrates me about having to prove who I am.

While finishing up my last two years of graduate school I worked on campus as a graduate assistant. My role allowed me to work with students, which is something that I truly enjoy. I worked with several students on campus but none became attached to me as much as Cedric did. I remember our first advising session very vividly. My hair was pulled back and I was dressed in an eclectic way, a style that is very familiar to me. Before I could get through my normal "getting to know you questions" Cedric interrupted by asking "what are you?" Amazed by his interruption and simple yet complex question I responded, "what do you mean what am I?" His jovial laugh accompanied by "you know, what is your race?" let me know that he was genuinely unaware.

After I politely told him that I was Black just like him he replied with "I know that but what else are you mixed with?" At this point I am bit confused and little on edge. We are supposed to be talking about him, not me. Also, it had been a while since I had been asked this question so I wondered what prompted him. After pointing out the fact that my hair was locked (an obvious identifier to me) I stated (probably a bit sarcastically) that my father was

Black and my mother is Black so that made me 100% Black. He chuckled and we began our advising session.

This conversation made me think of the documentary that Soledad O'Brian, a former CNN correspondent, did in 2012 entitled "Who is Black in America." In it she discusses the issue of colorism from the perspective of light skinned Black people. Like her, the people she interviewed were biracial and had lighter skin. As I watched the show I could connect with their issue of feeling casted out for not being Black enough, but I could not identify with their struggle of racial identity. In some ways this conversation on colorism approached in this way is a bit frustrating because I am persuaded to believe that people who are lighter because they are biracial and people who are lighter who have two Black parents have very different realities.

Thinking about my conversation with Cedric and looking back over my life I guess there are times where I could have "passed" for being biracial but never wanted to. This has nothing to do with whiteness and everything to do with my Blackness. I'm very proud to be Black and although I may share the same complexion with many biracial people, I believe that our struggles are different. I can't say whose struggles are more complicated and am not interested in discrediting any person's experience including my own, but what I can say is there needs to be space for all of us to heal. A big space because everyone needs it.

Cedric did not ask me many other questions beyond what I was. But the next student I encountered did. While in graduate school I had the opportunity to explore life in a way that I had not been able to before. During one spring semester I got heavily involved in the campus recreation program. I participated in several outdoor events (this is not something I ever thought I would do) and had an amazingly good time. One trip in particular, lake kayaking, was wonderful. I spent an entire day out on a lake with fellow Spartans learning how to

Kayak and learn about nature itself. Although I put sunblock on, as to not get burned, not to avoid a tan, it was undeniably warm on this particular day and I not only got a deep tan but also sun burned very badly. If I had it to do all over again though I wouldn't change a thing.

At work the following week I ran into one of the students who worked in our office. Calvin was very mature, thus all of the graduate students in the office had very candid conversations with him. As soon as he saw me he said "wow, somebody got a tan." I giggled and said "yes" I did and then he immediately followed up with "how does it feel to have color now?" I was taken back and slightly offended and replied with "What do you mean? I've always had color, I'm Black!" By the look in his eyes I could tell that he was not trying to offend me. He honestly had no way of knowing how triggering that could have been for me. I knew that his question was innocent. Still, it stung. I did not take time that day to explain my answer to him. I don't think he was mature enough to understand and looking back on it I wasn't mature enough to explain it.

I remember being very angry about it. I never liked to be challenged about my racial identity. As a more mature adult I know that I need to find the proper words to share with my children if or when they are faced with this same situation. It may not mean the same thing to them however as it does to me. If any of them do in fact have to have the conversation, I can only hope that it would not be in a way that they would have to defend who they are. I desire that their Blackness would not be gauged by who is more authentic and who is not.

## She Is a Real Sistah

Attending a Predominately White Institution (PWI) for the first time as a graduate student was a very new experience for me. I received all of my formal education in predominately Black spaces. While I was adjusting to the change in culture I often vis-

ited my collegiate alma mater, a Historically Black College/University (HBCU) to keep me grounded in a sense. Much like the student organization that I spoke about at the beginning of this chapter, my alma mater put on a similar program centered on colorism that I was able to attend. The room was crowded with students who wanted to explore a topic that had deeply touched so many of them.

The people on the panel appeared to be strategically placed by shade. I was not quite sure why this separation was necessary, or how or why those particular students were chosen but as you can imagine it bothered me. Most people's experiences with colorism are individual thus, one light brown skin person cannot speak for all light skinned people, nor can one medium brown skin person speak for all brown skinned people, nor can one dark brown skin person speak for all dark skinned people. Although there was a student panel the moderator, Dr. Allison, did the majority of the speaking.

In the back of the room sat the current Queen for the institution, whom was a light skinned young woman with natural hair. As Dr. Allison began to speak not only was I uncomfortable for her but was disturbed by her choice of stories. Unfortunately, she monopolized the floor which left little to no time for student voices to be heard. This validates my thoughts of all us really needing space for healing. She began to tell the story of the evolution of colorism on the college campus as she saw it. She could not believe that after all these years that the age-old topic had resurfaced and had done so with a vengeance. She proceeded with the talk that a young lady wanted to run to be the queen of the university but was afraid because she heard the queen had to be light skinned. Because Dr. Allison did, and had for many years, oversaw the queens of the institution, the young lady felt comfortable speaking with her concerning this. Not only did she reassure the student that was not true (a simple history of looking at the queens would have told her the same thing) she began to tell the young lady of a time when she remembered the queens of the college were "real sistahs."

She began to describe to the audience what this real sistah looked like. She said the queens who were real dark skinned, with afros were naturally beautiful. Her description of a real sistah alienated those Black women who did not look like that. She ended her story with a speech to the darker skinned sistahs telling them to not let anybody tell them they are not beautiful simply because they were dark. I completely agreed with her, but what advice did she have for the women who were not dark? What advice did she have for the Black women who, in her eyes, were not considered "real sistahs"? Where did they fit into the conversation? Where did they fit in that "safe space" of Blackness?

It is easy to see why Dr. Allison projected her feelings upon the students in the room. We see and experience the world through our own lenses. What is most complicated about the story is the feelings I felt when sitting in a shared space where affirmations were needed for everyone. The narrative should have been we are all one and no matter your complexion we share this gift and burden of Blackness. When I sat in those types of spaces before I felt the pain of my darker hue sistahs and suppressed my own pain. I felt that I did not have the right to take up that space. I was wrong. The hurt that is experienced by Black and Brown women as it relates to colorism is infinite. I wish I could say that it was only felt by women but unfortunately men experience it too.

## Divided Perception: They Like Him Better

I miss my days at my old university. My office was always filled with lots of students, laughter and talk. The days I enjoyed the most were the ones that students would come to my office just to hang out because they knew they would run into other student-athletes that they possibly had not seen in a while.

Many of them considered my office to be "home room." When it was several of them in there, they entertained each other, thus I was able to still get a lot of work done in their company. It was times like this when students had their most truthful conversations. I want to believe that it was in part because they felt comfortable in my presence, but more so because they partially thought I was not listening. Although I may not have responded, I heard everything the students had to say. Of all the conversations that took place in my office none stuck with me more than the one held between Kevin and Andrew, two football players.

Kevin and Andrew had been friends since their first year at the university. They did just about everything together as they played the same position on the field, offensive line. These guys, although big, are typically the sweetest and most caring men on the team, at least that has been my experience. Kevin was dark complexioned, and Andrew was lighter complexioned. In addition to playing football together they were bouncers at a local club. They began to talk about how the owner of the club was prejudiced. Obviously, this disturbed me if they believed this was true, because they continued to work there. Although they laughed about it, I could tell that it bothered the guys, especially Kevin. They talked about an instance where the guys were asked to wear shorts below the knees and how Andrew was allowed to wear whatever kind of shorts he wanted. They attributed this difference to their shades, although they previously stated that overall the manager was prejudiced.

After chiming into their conversation (I could not resist—it was about what I am passionate about) they told me that what their manager was doing was normal, because it all stemmed back to the "field negro" and the "house negro." Although Kevin and Andrew were both college students on full scholarships, and Kevin was actually the stronger student (more involved, a member of a Greek letter organization and overall more popular) in this one instance they blamed the difference on skin tone.

The old narrative about the field and house negro is often spoke of with great confidence. As I've discussed in previous chapters it is one that should be challenged for many reasons. The original idea of house negro versus field negro is completely different from the relaxed version of what people speak of in modern times. Once upon a time these terms had everything to do with a mentality and not a complexion. There is great danger in diluting meanings to words. It gives space for misinterpretation which ultimately leads to misunderstanding. In the instance of Kevin and Andrew I believe that what they experienced was very real. I'm glad that they focused on their similarities versus their differences. I wish more people were able to do this, including myself.

I almost experienced the same scenario one day while writing in a coffee shop. I met a Black man named Shawn who also dealt with colorism in his family. Much like my experience with most people of color, once I shared my research topic with him, he began to share his personal story with me as it relates to colorism.

Shawn was from the Midwest. He came to North Carolina to attend college. This is not as unique as his journey to how he got here. Shawn grew up in a rough neighborhood in Chicago, Illinois. He grew up with a twin brother. His brother was lighter complexioned, and Shawn was darker skinned. Sitting there watching him talk about the differences in complexions I could tell how hurtful some of his experiences were growing up. He shared that he felt his parents adorned his brother more. He felt that he always received better clothes and just more love from his family. It would have been interesting to speak with his brother and his parents to see if they too shared these same sentiments, but they weren't there, Shawn was. He was a stranger to me yet when the space was provided he opened up his deep wounds of colorism that he got from within his family.

Shawn's tone changed when he began to talk about the turn in his life. Although his brother was lighter complexioned he is now in prison doing time while Shawn is married with a wife and child and just completed his terminal degree. With a boyish grin he said that his brother was supposed to be the one with all of *this* because of how much love he got when they were younger but "I am the one who made it."

As Shawn came back to the present moment with his eyes and his thoughts, I couldn't help but wonder if he was happy that he was the one who "made it" or if he was shocked. It was unclear to me if he had any heartache about his brother being in jail. The one thing that was very clear was Shawn was dark skinned, his brother was light skinned (according to him) and that contrast had deeply shaped the way that Shawn viewed the world.

Like every encounter I have as it pertains to colorism, I'm left with more questions than answers. For example, did Shawn truly beat the odds of his skin color or did he beat the odds of a Black man in general? Was his brother really light skinned? How would his brother interpret their childhood and now their adulthood? Was Shawn really loved less by his parents because he was darker? I obviously don't have the answers to these questions, but I do have the answer to if colorism exists amongst men. The answer is yes but in different ways.

### I Am Light Skin Darn It!

In addition to being part of a Greek Panhellenic Sorority, I am also involved in an Academic Sisterhood called DIVAS, which stands for Divine, Intellectual, Virtuous, Academic Sistas. The overall purpose of DIVAS is to provide a community for women of color who are either in pursuit of their PhD or who have begun their journey into the academy. As a part of our community women are paired with other women (we refer to them as bigs and littles) as to keep a closer watch on each other. For a period of time in my PhD process I was what I like to call a "lost soul." I wanted my PhD but I allowed my life circumstances to overshadow my goals. After refocusing and getting back to what was most central and important to me, I resigned from my thriving position of eight years to pursue completing my degree. Although hard, the decision paid off and within a month's time I had made major steps towards finishing my degree. Being a former "lost soul" I take special interest in those who I feel may be a little lost themselves. As such I invited one my fellow DIVAS out to lunch to check in on her.

As we talked and caught up on the small things in life, Candice and I did what any and every graduate student and even former graduate student does. We began to talk about our experiences as graduate students and our research agendas. Like most people Candice found my topic to be very interesting. She began to talk about her husbands'experience and how he felt that he was brown skinned even though most people who saw him would agree that he is darker complexioned. I have seen her husband before and would agree with her on this one. Ironically he grew up in the same town that Natalie grew up in from Church. After we laughed a bit about his thoughts she began to tell me her thoughts on colorism.

There is no question that Candice would be considered to be brown skin by most people, but in her eyes she was much lighter. Much like her husband, she had internalized an identity that truly did not belong to her. She began to tell me of experiences that she felt that people discriminated against her because of her complexion. Although the research written shows that she would not be discriminated against because she was brown skinned, in her eyes she was lighter and it had been done. I could not believe that she had those experiences or that she considered herself light skinned but I heard her very loud and clear. Her words screamed "I am light skinned darn it!"

After meeting with her I thought about the program that Crystal had put on where students self-selected to enter groups based on their complexions but were denied access because of what others felt about them. I challenged my need to tell her that she was a different hue than what she believed herself to be. It made me turn to other stories of medium brown complexioned women only to learn that they too have experienced the trauma of colorism. This frightened me as much of what I believed to be true regarding the safety of medium brown skinned women was slipping away. The complexion that I saw as the glue, the safety net, the safe space for Black women was no longer there. An entire group of Black women had been tucked in a safe space in my mind and left out of the colorism trauma and I was happy for them. This conversation taught me that it was time for me to hear their voices. This led me to social media to find more personal narratives of women who may have felt the same way as Candice. What I found was more disturbing than what I already knew.

**#teamlightskin**

I joined X, formerly known as twitter, many years ago. My reasoning was simple. I work with college students, and although I never actually use my account, I do not want to be left behind the times. One day while on the application I came across several post that said #teamlightskin. At the time I had no idea that this was considered a trending topic for people to write about, although I was looking at several post from people across the country and possibly even the world. The post I read disturbed me deeply. It was light skinned girls writing about why they love being light skinned. Such things like "I can wear my hair any color" to "because everybody likes me" were written. More disturbing than the tweets were the post I saw from girls who were not light skinned, but who considered themselves to be so. Furthermore, the posts that were written about why being dark skinned was not cool truly broke me.

After researching more, I learned that not only was there a "team light skin," but "team dark skin" as well as "team brown skin". On one hand it seems logical to have great pride in your skin tone. On the other hand it feels divisive and dated. The fact that social media has created an outlet to further perpetuate the divide of colorism is problematic in itself. The fact that younger people are still subscribing to this way of thought is even more troubling. I believe that #teamBlack would be a better use of energy. This hashtag does exists but has nothing to do with actually being a Black person but rather the color Black in itself which is entirely another book all together.

## Conclusion

This chapter could have been the entire book as the conversations and experiences I have had over the years have been numerous. The stories I have shared are most likely no different from ones that you or others around you may have experienced. These encounters are the ones that have had the lasting impact on my journey through colorism thus far. Sharing these stories was not an easy task but in my desire to encourage others to have open and honest dialogue concerning colorism it was only befitting to begin that discourse in my own way. In full transparency I wrote this book for Black and Brown girls but I also secretly desired that white folk read it as well. Not for any other reason than finding more depth and understanding to the daily struggles that Black people have because of the overwhelming and for some all consuming residual effects of racism.

There are risks however when having these types of conversations with people outside of my marginalized race. For starters you never want anyone to develop the notion that Black people are racist to one another thus diluting what it means to really be racist. If you are reading this and think that please let me help you out. That is not possible. Colorism is systemic from racism. Black people do not have the power to be racist. They can socially discriminate against other people who are not Black. They can hold strong negative opinions about people who are white. They can even go as far as individually hating people from another race. All of this and more can happen and it still does not make them racist. To be racist one must have power over another group of people on a macro level. Historically and to date that type of power only belongs to one group of people. The same group of people who have historically benefited from racism.

Experiencing the residual effects of something that continues to perpetuate the division amongst communities of color is exhausting. Reliving these stories and telling them to others however has been empowering. Concealing our stories and our trauma and only keeping them to ourselves validates them as if they are normal. Holding that pain to ourselves is unhealthy and in some ways stabilizes the power of the dominant culture. Fighting amongst each other about which skin type is better or worse lessens the responsibility of the white race as it pertains to the topic of racism.

In the beginning of this chapter, I provided seven themes that most commonly emerge from other readings on colorism as well as my personal experience with the topic. In the realm of colorism it is universally understood that a Black person of lighter hue will have an overall better quality of life in these areas simply because of their skin tone and likeness to white. The complexity of colorism being systemic from racism however challenges this notion because when it is all said done a light skinned or brown skin Black person for this matter is still Black. How can one person be privileged and oppressed for the same exact identity? My final chapter will explore this concept and much more.

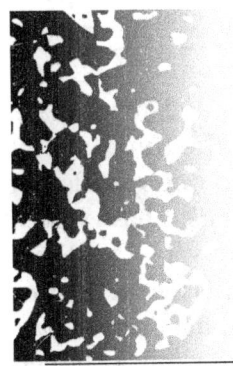

CHAPTER FIVE

# You Can't Stay in The Past So How Do We Move Forward: Education as a Form of Liberation

In this book I have discussed the sensitive issue of race and racism in America. My conversation on this topic led me to a deeper discussion on colorism and how it has affected my life. Historically within the Black race people have adopted a belief in the hierarchy system which privileges lighter skin over darker skin. In fact, the definition that most people subscribe to states just that. In this final chapter I would like to offer a definition that fully speaks to this phenomenon and gives space for all Black people to heal. Colorism negatively affects everyone not just women of a darker hue. The victimization is felt by all. How we make sense of this victimization is what will bring us through this trauma together.

Throughout the years internalized racism has remained alive through generational trauma. Over the years the terms such as "house negro" versus

"field negro" were used to describe and divide Black folk from each other. Although the initial use of these terms was not connected to one's shade but rather their mentality over the years it has evolved to now mean just that. The modern version of these words can be found in terms such as team light or team dark skin and a new one that has evolved over the years and that is team brown skin. Although many people find points of pride in these "teams" there are many instances where negative stereotypes are attached to each one. Furthermore, they deepen the divide and further perpetuate this division amongst Black people.

So, the question remains: Can a person be privileged for the same identity that they are oppressed for? Because, after all, that is the complex idea that current definitions of colorism are suggesting. Let us explore multiple identities by first examining the socially constructed idea of race that has led to the excruciating pain of racism. When we speak of racism it can be universally understood that it is prejudice, discrimination, or antagonism directed against a person or people based on their membership in a particular racial or ethnic group, typically one that is minority or marginalized. In this a person who is white is privileged for their skin and a person who is non-white is not. There is no gray area with this. It is important to focus on the minority or marginalized in this particular definition and to note that it is referring to minority in power and marginalized historically. Again, think about the definition on a macro level. This should help with any doubt or confusion one may have about individual experiences with race. For example, a white person saying something such as "on my job I am the only white person so I'm the minority and therefore people can be racist to me." That's an individual experience and not cumulative of the experiences that are felt on the larger scale within society. When that person goes to the grocery store for example the privilege of their skin is still available. I'm not denying that someone could not experience hurtful and wrongful encounters from a person of a minority or marginalized race. I'm simply stating that those experiences don't speak to the definition of racism.

Now let's add another example to the identity, sexism, which is linked to the belief that [wo]men and men should operate in specific roles in society. These roles typically rank one gender as superior to another and generally isolates those persons who do not identify as neither or both. There is clear power between who is privileged and who is not and persons who are not privileged can never gain the power for the same identity that they are oppressed for.

If we went through all of the major identities, we would clearly see who is oppressed and who is privileged. And with these identities a person can typically not be privileged for the very identity that they are oppressed for. For example, using the identities from above, a Black cisgender man would be privileged for being a man but oppressed for being Black. In this instance he does experience both power and lack thereof however it is not for the same identity. Now let's add to the conversation that he is a light skinned Black man. The definition of colorism as we now understand it would state that he now has privilege. So, my question: is how far does this privilege extend to the outside world? Do those who operate in power and privilege perceive his life any differently because he has light skin or is he still seen and treated as a Black man and all that may mean to society? I believe that a careful look at the history of Black men in America will answer this. The nuisance of colorism however manifests itself differently with Black men than it does with Black women but using this example was the easiest way to illustrate the point I am making as Black women are both oppressed for being Black and for being a woman.

The notion that skin tone stratification is not just about the shade of one's skin but rather about the bigger system of oppression should not be missed in this conversation. This system causes people who have shared origins to divide amongst each other. This divisive nature was inherited from racism and has penetrated the minds of so many. It is impossible to talk about colorism without racism. A definition that speaks to the collective trauma of Black people and allows space for everyone on the spectrum to heal should read as such. Colorism is a form of internalized racism that causes division within Black and Brown communities. People of all shades are affected by this tragic phenomenon. For years the focus has been on the long suffering of darker hue individuals while other shades have suffered in silence. In the same way that Black people have unified against racism so is the need to do so with colorism. It is an endemic plague that has lasted far too long.

In 2012, a former CNN reporter Soledad O'Brian (2012) hosted *Who is Black in America?* The documentary was the fifth one of the multi-part series which discussed the idea of Blackness in this country. In it, Soledad spoke to the idea of colorism through the perspective of light skinned biracial people. Although I am not biracial, I could identify with many of the struggles because many of them were because of the "shade" of their skin.

O'Brian followed the lives of several young people who struggled with colorism on a daily basis. For them the idea of Blackness was not as definitive as it may be to others. This is due to the complexion of their skin. Nayo Jones, a 17-year-old who was part of the documentary stated "they always called me white girl. I was never ashamed of myself until they taught me to be ashamed." Placing Nayo's struggle and others like herself, at the forefront of the documentary allowed the issue of colorism to be discussed from a different perspective that is not normally investigated.

This documentary allowed for the exploration of being a lighter shade as it relates to being Biracial which I believe to be a completely different experience from being lighter complexion individual and having two Black parents. Often I have been asked if I was Biracial and seemingly forced to understand the struggles of those who are because we may share a similar complexion. To that I have always shared that I believe our experiences are different. I don't struggle between races. I struggle within one. This is not stated to lessen the burden that anyone feels. I am simply speaking from my own experience.

It was reported that the series *Who is Black in America* has been one of the most watched shows on CNN since it first aired in September 2008. The popularity of the show would suggest that there is in interest in wanting to understand what it means to be Black in America more. Understanding is the beginning of all change. There have been other documentaries which have sought to speak to this issue of Blackness, which also addressed colorism; none however have reached such mainstream appeal.

**Golden**

Although I did not agree with all that was written in her book, I have Marita Golden (2004) to thank for giving me the courage to do this work. Her life and her story have been a true inspiration for me. The moment I knew that I could do what I was attempting to do was when I read the following passage.

> Writing about the color complex means thinking about the color complex, and the process becomes akin to breaking through a dense, evil encryption that masks, hides, denies, and silences the truth about what we have inflicted on ourselves. Writing this book, *I surrender to memory*. Writing this book, I inevitably seek out and find others brave enough to witness, question, and remember. (2004, p. 53)

In this book I began to surrender to my own memories. I certainly had to be brave. I witnessed, questioned, remembered and now I challenge you to do the same.

Even though Golden and I share a difference of opinion, I recognize that this is due in majority to our age difference, geographical regions and of course our skin tone. Each has given us a very different meanings of colorism. One thing is certain, we both have had to deal (I am still dealing) with it in our own way. My journey through colorism healing has now taken a different turn as I am experiencing and anticipating it through the lives of my children, specifically my daughters.

Since I began my initial steps in my journey there have been several works that have been added to the conversation. I most value Golden's still however because of her personal connection to the work. She is my muse. To study a phenomenon from afar is very different than to live through a phenomenon up close. Through her work I found frustration. I found perspective. I found purpose. I found my own voice.

## Liberation through Education

"To be changed by ideas was pure pleasure. But to learn ideas that ran counter to values and beliefs learned at home was to place oneself at risk, to enter the danger zone" (hooks, 1994, p. 3). This danger zone, is what I felt I entered once I began to formulate and verbalize my truth about what I have experienced. To be honest I still feel like I'm in this zone but in order for me to grow, I had to seek more knowledge about the very thing that was binding me. In chapter four, I shared that I learned about colorism at home. I never learned that others were "bad" because of their shade or that I was "good" I just knew that I was different. By no means did I understand while standing in the circle getting ready to fight all those years ago why I was always told *"you think you are cute because you are light skin"* was connected to colorism but as I got older, I realized the kids I was fighting were only saying what they heard from their families. And those adults in those families learned it from those who were once their elders. I don't think they understood it either. Yet still we all felt the pain.

Society teaches us about racism but through our actions and beliefs we perpetuate it through internalized racism. This is no fault of our own. Our educational spaces need to be used as platforms where people can discover their own truths. I am not just referring to education in a traditional sense, but rather education in a holistic way. Shapiro (2006) reflects:

> Education refers to the whole process of socialization that includes all those things and influences that shape how we think, act and relate to the world we live in. This certainly includes school, but it also includes other powerful influences on us, such as the family, peer relationships, religious institutions, popular culture, and the mass media. (p. 52)

This type of education is critical and necessary when it comes to internalized racism, which some see as the new "ism". In our *modern* times I'd say it is not so new to many but the continued quest to understand it while never forgetting that is directly connected to racism is critically important. Spaces need to be created which will allow people to truly deal with this topic. I can see this happening successfully in our community, our classrooms (making them culturally relevant) and finally through media opportunities.

### Community

Much of the liberation that has happened throughout the years for Black people has happened in the church. "The Black church is where Black folks go when grief-ridden" (Cooper-Lewter, 1999, p. 8). In previous eras, such as the civil rights movement, churches were used as the hub where people went to resolve collective issues (Gadzekpo, 1997). Al-

though the Black community is no longer the way it was during the 1960s, many Black people find church as a resting place to lay their own personal struggles down. "The common Black argument for belief in God is not that it is logical or reasonable, but rather that such belief is requisite for one's sanity and for entrée to the most uplifting sociality available in the Black community" (West, 1999, p. 437).

The issue of internalized racism is a struggle that I have had to deal with. If you can remember, from chapter four, Natalie struggled with it as well, as does Golden. Each of us are three various shades but we all struggle. I know that we are not the only ones. Finding a community of others who either struggle or seek understating regarding this issue is critical for collective healing.

> The community enables us to see our own life as something much more than an isolated, brief moment of consciousness simply here to satisfy our egoistical wants. Within this community of meaning I can see my own life as a continuing link in a chain that connects me to countless others who have felt similar responsibilities, perceived and attended to similar challenges and experienced, celebrated, or commemorated familiar events and moments with similar rituals. (Shapiro, 2006, p. 80)

It is in these collective spaces where we are able to set aside our differences in hope for a better tomorrow. The key is to actively listen more than you speak and to speak with intention.

## Culturally Relevant Classrooms

Culturally relevant learning spaces need to be created for those people who have the opportunity to confront skin tone stratification in traditional learning environments. Ladson-Billings (2009a) asserts that culturally relevant teaching is:

*a pedagogy of opposition* not unlike critical pedagogy but specifically committed to collective, not merely individual, empowerment. Culturally relevant pedagogy rests on three criteria or propositions:(a) Students must experience academic success; (b) students must develop and/or maintain cultural competence; and (c) students must develop a critical consciousness through which they *challenge the status quo* of the current social order. (p. 160)

Classrooms where students are only deposited in and not encouraged to discuss and challenge what they have learned needs to be a thing of the past. Because racism is overt and covert culturally relevant spaces will allow room for all people, regardless of their race or shade, to be successful.

Students must be given the space to critique ideas and identities which are associated with them as well as others. In questioning the norms, they have the opportunity to become free of what they expect of themselves and people around them. This type of freedom Freire (2004) explains:

> is acquired by conquest not by gift. *It must be pursued constantly and responsibly.* Freedom is not an ideal located outside of man; nor is it an idea which becomes myth. It is rather the indispensable condition for the quest for human completion. (p. 47)

This type of freedom of thought does not come naturally, especially since students have been taught all of their lives to not question knowledge. It is the responsibility of the teacher, the facilitator, the guider of knowledge, to not only encourage academic success and cultural competence but most importantly help students recognize, understand and critique social inequalities (Ladson-Billings, 1995). We must enter each learning space understanding that it will bring new challenges for our students as well as ourselves. We must also learn to be okay with that. Culturally relevant classrooms require openness from both the student and the teacher, but the teacher must model the behavior first.

**Media Responsibility**

When one is not in control of her image what she sees is essentially considered fiction. Only when one can become in control of what she sees can it reflect actuality, a form of art; perhaps something that she can even see as beautiful. "Films possess the ability to *re-imagine* and *refocus* what American culture knows to be 'real,' particularly pertaining to Black culture" (McKoy, 2012, p. 135). Challenging the way we receive stereotypical images that are depicted through movies is one idea. Actually, having the space to alter what is seen is something totally different.

Although there are Black screenwriters and producers in Hollywood there are not enough to change the influence of what is seen. There is one producer however, Tyler Perry, who has crossed over to mainstream appeal. Unfortunately, he is known to overtly perpetuate the stereotype of Blackness especially Black women (Harrison, 2009; McKoy, 2012). Because of this "critics have vociferously condemned Perry's representations of face in his films and television shows" (Patterson, 2011, p. 10). Some feel that his portrayal of Blackness, in particular, Black women, is the reason he has been so successful in reaching audiences outside of the Black community. Although he is very popular many have criticized his work, wondering if he "is capable or even willing to disrupt negative media stereotypes of African Americans and challenge this system of American cultural hegemony" (Harrison, 2009, p. 108). Even though he has publicly spoken of being aware of the past stereotypes of Black people, his movies still perpetuate the three stereotypical roles of mammy, sapphire, and jezebel that were created many years ago. Spike Lee has openly spoken out against Tyler Perry's movies. Regrettably, some people see it as jealousy rather than a political stance.

I personally have felt torn between being overly entertained by his main character Madea, an overzealous Black Grandmother and being repulsed by another Black man rising to fame using a stereotypical depiction of a Black woman. There are too many male actors to name who have done this. Perry, however made history in 2019 by opening up Tyler Perry Studios in Southwest Atlanta making him the first African American to outright own the largest major film production studio. With his recent release of *A Jazzman's Blues* (2022) one could only hope that he plans to elevate the image of a Blackness through characters that show the fullness of the Black experience. One thing is for certain and that is he has the power to do so in a way that many of his critics do not. In addition to Perry, Tammy Williams is a majority owner of a new television studio in Atlanta which puts her in major position to help sculpt the master narrative of Black women.

Another prominent producer of Black film is Bishop T. D. Jakes. Although a Bishop of one of the largest mega-ministries in the USA, Jakes (2013) states, "I realized that there are more people in the theater on Friday and Saturday night than there are in the pews on Sunday morning" (as cited in A. Williams, 2013, p. 3), which is why he began to produce movies. In doing so Jakes has crossed over from church appeal to worldly appeal. Bishop Jakes states that his messages are portrayed to help people through their struggles. Be it true (or not depending on your opinion) his 2012 film, *Sparkle,* clearly perpetuated the stereotypes of colorism and Black identity. Sparkle, a light skinned girl is the superstar of the movie. Her dark skinned sister, Carmen, is a troublemaker and her other light skinned sister, Delores, is a sexy songstress who seduced men. In watching the movie, it is easy to see how colorism exists.

With many producers of Black films, both Black and white, but very few who are willing to challenge the stereotypes, we as a people are left with an insurmountable obstacle of internalized racism.

But still there must be hope. If we teach ourselves, as well as our younger generation, to challenge what is seen and not accept it as face value, then at least we have started somewhere. The bigger challenge is to continue to put pressure on producers, both Black and white by publicly using our voice to speak out against what is seen. This position holds true for producers of reality television and social media platforms as well.

**Intergroup Dialogue**

My final offering of ways to make peace or find resolve with colorism is intergroup dialogue. In discussing race too often conversations are just about Black and white. Although people of color in general interact with one another, there usually is not a shared space where issues of internalized oppressions, such as colorism, can be discussed. Intergroup dialogue (IGD), which is *guided* facilitation, I believe can be used as a place to create this space. IGD would bring Black women face-to-face and give them a "safe space" to challenge and discuss this very sensitive issue.

Intergroup dialogues are defined as facilitated face-to-face meetings between students from two or more social identity groups that have history of conflict or potential conflict (Nagda & Zúñiga, 2003). It is more than just a simple dialogue, but rather a *guided discussion* between people. Intergroup dialogue originated on a college campus as a response to tough issues of social inequalities.

Two trained facilitators lead the discussion and should represent two identities that are represented within the group. The group needs to be reasonably small. An example for IGD for colorism would be two people of different hues serving as the lead facilitators. These persons must be trained and grounded in creating and fostering a safe space for difficult conversations. They must also have enough emotional maturity to withstand the challenging discussions ahead.

Intergroup Dialogue is different from a regular conversation because there are goals, learning outcomes and facilitated discussions. Because people have to sign up for IGD sessions, there is a higher probability that they are open to talk. Understanding that the issues of racism and colorism are very sensitive for many it could be presumed that anger and frustration would be part of the experience. Anger is not a bad emotion. In fact, too often Black women are silenced (indirectly and directly) out of fear of being labeled the "angry Black woman." This space would welcome this emotion and use it to further the transformative experiences that are needed. Intergroup dialogue usually takes place outside of traditional academic settings. I would be remiss if I did not mention that if a Black woman is angry she probably has every right to be I did not mention that if a Black woman is angry she probably has every right to be.

**Journaling**

Last but certainly not least is journaling. This will provide a safe space for those who may be struggling with the idea of colorism to get their emotions outside of their own minds. A step further would be to share these ideas with others. Everyone has a very different process when they journal but for those who may not know where to start, I would like to offer you a few writing prompts to assist you. Consider answering the following:

1. The first time I experienced colorism was . . .
2. If I had to sum up colorism in my own words, I would say . . .
3. Thinking about colorism makes me feel . . . .
4. I'd like to talk about colorism with ___ because . . . .
5. I'd like to explore ___ as it pertains to colorism.

When journaling consider being free with your ideas and thoughts. Don't worry about perfection or what others may think. Unless you want them to nobody will ever see your words. Focus on being honest with yourself. Reflect on your experiences and how they made you feel. Write until you feel like your work is done and when you are ready write some more. Journaling is a process. Be patient with yourself.

## Conclusion

There was a time in my life when discussing colorism would evoke such strong emotions in me that I would find myself on the defense. Many years later however I understand that the pain I felt and oftentimes still feel is not the responsibility of anyone around me but rather the ugly roots of racism. Writing this book has allowed me to be reflective in a way that has brought healing to my life and made space for me to encourage others to do the same.

Oftentimes when people are in oppressive situations, they find it difficult to get past what they see. It is usually the ways in which we are marginalized that are most salient to us. The ways in which our identities may marginalize others is not as easily seen or acceptable. It takes a lot of introspective reflection to get to a place where we are able to not only see the ways in which we are oppressed or have been oppressed but also how we may have identities, they have oppressed others. It is finding this balance that can lead one to viewing the world in a more holistic way; loving thy neighbor as they wish to be loved and loving thy self as you need to be loved.

We need collective healing as it pertains to colorism. The internalized notion that any shade is better than one shade because it is closer to white is toxic. Setting value on one's beauty based on European standards is an antiquated thought. Furthermore, Black women being awarded for roles that further perpetuate the stereotypes of mammy, sapphire and jezebel weakens and threatens the collective identity of Black women. None of us, dark brown, medium brown or light brown feel good when we are marginalized because of our skin. None of us should feel good when we are pitted against each other. The key is not to continue to see race, racism and colorism as a separate issue but rather understanding that each exists together and are fundamentally destructive to the Black race. It is time to begin to have these conversations with people who look like us and with people who don't. Internalized racism is not just a Black person's problem for if one of us amongst has an issue then we all do.

Through education we have the ability to reform communities and find new meaning for our moral and spiritual lives (Shapiro, 2006). The hidden curriculum of race, racism and colorism has been a part of who we are but does not have to define us. This process has taught me this. Education has provided a space where I could begin to understand the ideas and images that I have been presented through media, as well as given me a place where I could learn to accept or reject these images. I choose to reject them. I understand that not all people will have the opportunity to engage in education in the way that I have (I do recognize my privilege in this) but I do suggest, as hooks, Shapiro, Greene, Knowles, and others have that education is the space that you make it. And much like Paulo Freire shared in his work I believe that education can be used as a form of liberation to free people from their internalized oppressions.

Popular culture has an enormous influence on informing who we are to ourselves, as well as whom we are to others. It is our reasonable obligation to not enact that which we see if it is not who we are. I do understand that if it were as easy as rejecting ideas then race, racism and colorism would have ended so many years ago and there would not have been a need for this book. Still, we must be aware of the ways in which these *isms* have become a mainstay in our society. We must challenge them at every juncture and must find our voices in spaces that otherwise have chosen to speak for us.

My hope for the future is more collaborations and ways in which Blackness can be discussed and celebrated. There are many sistahs out there who are doing this work already. I would encourage you to find them and your space at the table. If you don't like the table that is before you create one. I once wrote that I looked forward to the day that we could possibly transcend the idea of race. I no longer feel this way. I believe my race is such a strong part of my identity that removing myself from it would be like separating me from the air that I breathe. Instead, I hope for the day that we can understand the intricate nuisances of race, racism and colorism in America and that we can move openly and honestly through what we each discover. I have my own children, nieces, nephews, and little cousins who are depending on us to do so.

Now that I am at the end of this work, I feel a greater sense of understanding and peace. Unlike the woman who once believed that I did not have the right to share my story as a light brown, Black woman I now have more understanding and empathy for my own trauma and past experiences. I fear less what others may think of this work and hope more for what it may evoke in them. Those who don't write are written for. Those who don't speak are spoken for. Use your voice and when you feel courageous enough share it with the world.

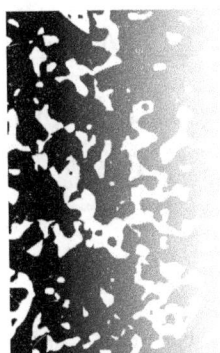

# Bibliography

Adams, M. (2000). Conceptual frameworks. In M. Adams, W. J. Blumenfeld, R. Castaneda, H. W. Hackman, M. L. Peters, & X. Zuniga (Eds.), *Readings for diversity and social justice: An anthology on racism, antisemitism, sexism, heterosexism, ableism, and classism* (pp. 5–9). New York, NY: Routledge.

Adams, M., Blumenfeld, W. J., Castaneda, R., Hackman, H. W., Peters, M. L., & Zúñiga, X. (2000). *Readings for diversity and social justice: An anthology on racism, antisemitism, sexism, heterosexism, ableism, and classism* (pp. 457–469). New York, NY: Routledge.

African Holocaust. (2001). Retrieved March 22, 2012, from http://www.africanholocaust.net/news_ah/willielynch.htm

American Psychological Association. (2009). *Publication manual of the American Psychological Association* (6th ed.). Washington, DC: Author.

Andersen, M. L., Hill Collins, P. (1998). Race, Class, and Gender: An Anthology. United Kingdom: Wadsworth Publishing Company.

Ashby, L. (2006). *With amusement for all: A history of American popular culture since 1830.* Lexington, KY: The University Press of Kentucky.

Baldwin, J. (1984). *Notes of a native son.* Boston, MA: Beacon Press.

Bates, K., & Hudson, K. (1996). *The new basic Black-home training for modern times* (Rev. ed.). New York, NY: Doubleday.

Bishop, W. (1999). *Ethnographic writing research: Writing it down, writing it up, and reading it.* Portsmouth, NH: Boynton/Cook Publishers.

Blumenfeld, W. J., & Raymond, D. (2000). Prejudice and discrimination. In W. J. Blumenfeld, R. Castaneda, H. W. Hackman, M. L. Peters, & X. Zúñiga (Eds.), *Readings for diversity and social justice: An anthology on racism, antisemitism, sexism, heterosexism, ableism, and classism* (pp. 21–30). New York, NY: Routledge.

Boggs, J., & Petrie, D. (2008). *The art of watching films* (7th ed.). New York, NY: McGraw-Hill.

Bogle, D. (2001). *Toms, coons, mulattoes, mammies & bucks: An interpretive history of Blacks in American films.* New York: NY: Continuum.

Bogle, D. (2007). *Brown sugar.* New York: NY: Continuum.

Bonilla-Silva, E. (2006). *Racism without racist: Color-blind racism and the persistence of racial inequality in the United States.* Lanham, MD: Rowman & Littlefield.

Burke, P. J. (2006). *Contemporary social psychological theories.* Stanford, CA: Stanford University Press.

Burton, L., Bonilla-Silva, E., Ray, V., Budkelew, R., & Freeman, E. H. (2010). Critical race theories, colorism, and the decade's research on families of color. *Journal of Marriage and Family 72*, 440–459. doi:10.1111/j.1741-3737.2010.00712.x

Byfield, J., Denzer, L., & Morrison, A. (2010). *Gendering the African diaspora: Women, culture, and historical change in the Caribbean and Nigerian hinterland.* Bloomington, IN: Indiana University Press.

Casey, K. (1993). *I answer with my life: Life histories of women teachers working for social change.* New York, NY: Routledge.

Cashmore, E. (2010). Buying Beyoncé. *Celebrity Studies, 1*(2), 135–150. doi:10.1080/`939237.2010.482262

Chang, H. (2008). *Autoethnography as method.* Walnut Creek, CA: Left Coast Press.

Collins, P. H. (2000). *Black feminist thought: Knowledge, consciousness, and the politics of empowerment* (2nd ed.). New York, NY: Routledge.

Collins, P. H. (2005). *Black sexual politics: African Americans, gender, and the new racism.* New York & London: Routledge.

Columbus, C., Barnathan, M., Green, B. (Producer), & Taylor, T. (Director). (2011). *The help.* United States: DreamWorks Studios through Touchstone Pictures.

Cooper-Lewter, N. (1999). *Black grief and soul therapy.* Richmond, VA: Harriet Tubman Press.

Crenshaw, K., Gotanda, N., Pellar, G., & Thomas, K. (1996). *Critical race theory: The key writer that formed the movement.* New York, NY: New Press.

Cureton, S. R. (2002). An assessment of Wilson and Frazier's perspective on race and racial life chances. *African-American Research Perspectives, 8*(1), 47–54.

Daniels, L. (Producer), & Forster, M. (Director). (2001). *Monster's ball* (Motion Picture). United States: Lionsgate.

# Bibliography

Daniels, L., Magness, G., Siegel-Magness, S., Winfrey, O., Heller, T., Perry, T. (Producers), & Daniels, L. (Director). (2009). *Precious*. United States: Lionsgate.

Delgado, R., & Stefancic, J. (2001). *Critical race theory: An introduction*. New York & London: New York University Press.

Denzin, N. (1997). *Interpretive ethnography—ethnographic practices for the 21st century*. Thousand Oaks, CA: Sage.

Denzin, N., & Lincoln, Y. S. (2011). *The sage handbook of qualitative research*. Thousand Oaks, CA: Sage.

Dyer, R. (1988). White: The last "special" issue on race?. Screen, 29, 44-64.

Dill, K. (2009). *How fantasy becomes reality: Seeing through media influence*. New York, NY: Oxford.

Dyson, M. (2008). *April 4, 1968: Martin Luther King, Jr's death and how it changed America*. New York, NY: Basic Civitas Books.

Ellis, C. (1995). *Final negotiations: A story of love, loss, and chronic illness*. Philadelphia, PA: Temple University Press

Ellis, C. (1998). I hate my voice: Coming to terms with bodily stigmas. *The Sociological Quarterly, 39*, 517–537.

Ellis, C. (2004). *The ethnographic I: A methodological novel about autoethnography*. Walnut Creek, CA: Altamira Press.

Ellis, C., & Bouchner, A (2000). Autoethnography, personal narrative, reflexivity: Researcher as subject. In N. K. Denzin & Y. S. Lincoln (Eds.), *Handbook of qualitative research* (pp. 733–768). Thousand Oaks, CA: Sage Publications.

Etherington, K. (2004). *Becoming a reflexive researcher: Using our selves in research*. Philadelphia, PA: Jessica Kingsley Publishers.

Finkelman, P. (2010). *Milestone documents in African American history: Exploring the essential primary sources* (vol. 1). Dallas, TX: Schlager Group.

Finlay, L. (2002). Negotiating the swamp: The opportunity and challenge of reflexivity in practice. *Qualitative Research, 2*(2), 209–230. Retrieved from http://www.utsc.utoronto.ca/~kmacd/IDSC10/Readings/Positionality/reflex-2.pdf

Fleeson, W., & Wilt, J. (2010). The relevance of big five trait content in behavior to subject authenticity: Do high levels of within-person behavioral variability undermine or enable authenticity achievement? *Journal of Personality, 78*(4), 1353–1382. doi:10.1111/j.1467-6494.210.00653.x

Forbes, J. (1993). *Africans and Native Americans: The language of race and the evolution of red-Black peoples*. Chicago, IL: University of Illinois Press.

Four Arrows. (2008). *The authentic book: Alternative ways of knowing, research, and representation*. New York, NY: Routledge.

Freire, P. (2004). *Pedagogy of the oppressed* (30th anniversary ed.). New York, NY: Continuum.

Gadzekpo, L. (1997). The Black church, the civil rights movement, and the future. *Journal of Religious Thought, 53/54*(2/1), 95–112. Retrieved from http://connection.ebscohost.com/c/articles/1857238/Black-church-civil-rights-movement-future

Gainor, K. A. (2008). Internalized oppression as a barrier to effective group work with Black women. *The Journal for Specialist in Group Work, 17*(4), 235–242. doi:10.1080/01933929208414355

Gallagher, C. (2009). *Rethinking the color line readings in race and ethnicity* (4th ed.). Boston, MA: McGraw Hill

Gates, Jr., H. (1995). *Colored people: A memoir.* New York, NY: Vintage Books.

Glenn, E. (2009). *Shades of difference—Why skin color matters.* Stanford, CA: University Press.

Goldberg, W. (1991, March, 25). *Information revolution video file.* Retrieved from http://www.youtube.com/watch?v=-9kDwdxVlEw

Golden, M. (2004). *Don't play in the sun—one woman's journey through the color complex.* New York, NY: Random House.

Grason, S. (2005). *Journaloution: Journaling to awaken your inner voice, heal your life, and manifest your dreams.* Novato, CA: New World Library.

Graves, J. (2005). *The race myth: Why we pretend race exists in America.* New York, NY: Plume.

Greener, I. (2011). *Designing social research: A guide for the bewildered.* Los Angeles, CA: Sage.

Hall, R. (2005). The Euro-Americanization of race: Alien perspective of African Americans vis-á-vis trivialization of skin color. *Journal of Black Studies, 36,* 116–128. doi:10.1177/0021934704268297

Harris, T. (1982). *From mammies to militants: Domestics in Black American literature.* Philadelphia, PA: Temple University Press.

Harrison, T. (2009). Tyler Perry's *Madea Goes to Jail:* Normalizing hegemony and stereotypes of "Black crime." *McNair Scholars Journal, 13*(1), 107–120. Retrieved from http://www.csus.edu/McNair/Cohort_Journals_and_Photos/13_2011_2012/journal_2011-12/Theodore_Harrison_III.pdf

Harro, B. (2000). The cycle of socialization. In M. Adams, W. J. Blumenfeld, R. Castaneda, H. W. Hackman, M. L. Peters, & X. Zuniga (Eds.), *Readings for diversity and social justice: An anthology on racism, antisemitism, sexism, heterosexism, ableism, and classism* (pp. 15–20). New York, NY: Routledge.

Heider, K. (2006). *Ethnographic film* (Rev. ed.). United States of America: University of Texas Press.

Henderson, W. (2002). What's the difference between Willie Lynch, crabs in a barrel and Lenora Fulani? *New York Amsterdam News, 93*(39), 12.

Hesse-Biber, S. N. (2007). Exploring the interconnections of epistemology, methodology, and method. In S. N. Hesse-Biber (Ed.),

*Handbook of feminist research theory and practice* (pp. 1-26) Thousand Oaks, CA: Sage.

Hill, M. (2002). Skin color and the perception of attractiveness among African Americans: Does gender make a difference? *Social Psychology Quarterly, 65*(1), 77-91.

Hipolito-Delgado, C. (2010). Exploring the etiology of ethnic self-hatred: Internalized racism in Chicana/o and Latina/o college students. *Journal of College Student Development, 51*(3), 319-331.

Holliday, A. (2002). *Doing and writing qualitative research.* London: Sage.

Holloway, W., & Jefferson, T. (2000). *Doing qualitative research differently.* London: Sage Publications.

Holt, T. (1998). W. E. B. Dubois archaeology of race: Re-reading "the conservation of races." In M. Katz & T. Surge (Eds.), *W.E.B. Dubois, race, and the city: The Philadelphia negro and its legacy* (pp. 61-76). Philadelphia, PA: University of Pennsylvania.

hooks, b. (1994). *Teaching to transgress—education as the practice of freedom.* New York, NY: Routledge.

hooks, b. (2003). The oppositional gaze: Black female spectators. In Jones, A. (Ed.), *The Feminism and visual culture reader* Jones, A. (pp. 94-104). New York, NY: Routledge.

Howard, J. (1996). Hallelujah!: Transformation in film. *African American Review, 30*(3), 441-451.

Hunter, M. (2005). *Race, gender, and the politics of skin tone.* New York, NY and London: Routledge.

Kawash, S. (1996). The autobiography of an ex-coloured man: (Passing for) Black passing for white. In E. Ginsberg (Ed.), *Passing and the fictions of identity* (pp. 59-74). United States: Duke University Press.

Keith, V., & Herring, C. (1991). Skin tone and stratification in the Black community. *American Journal of Sociology, 97*(3), 760-778.

Kretsedemas, P. (2010). But she's not Black!: Viewer interpretations of 'angry Black women' on prime time TV. *Journal of African American Studies, 14,* 149-170. doi:10.1007/s1211-009-9116-3

Ladson-Billings, G. (1995). Toward a theory of culturally relevant pedagogy. *American Educational Research Journal, 32*(3), 465-491. doi:10.3102/00028312032003465

Ladson-Billings, G. (2009a). But that's just good teaching! The case for culturally relevant pedagogy. *Theory Into practice, 34*(3), 159-165. doi:10.1080/00405849509543675

Ladson-Billings, G. (2009b). "Who you callin' nappy-headed?": A critical race theory look at the construction of Black women. *Race Ethnicity and Education, 12*(1), 87-99. doi:10.1080/13613320802651012

Ladson-Billings, G. (2010). Just what is critical race theory and what's it doing in a nice field like education? *International Journal of Qualitative Studies in Education, 11*(1), 7-24. doi:10.1080/095183998236863

Ladson-Billings, G., & Tate, W. (1994). Toward a theory of critical race theory in education. *Teachers College Record, 97,* 47-68.

Lee, S., & Jones, L. (1988). *Uplift the race—the construction of school daze*. New York, NY: Simon & Schuster.

Maddox, K. (2004). Perspective on racial phenotypicality bias. *Personality and Social Psychology Review, 8*(4), 383–401.

Mask, M. (2009). *Divas on screen: Black women in American film*. Urbana and Chicago, IL: University of Illinois Press.

McKoy, B. (2012). Tyler Perry and the weight of misrepresentation. *McNair Scholars Research Journal, 5*(1), art. 10. Retrieved from http://commons.emich.edu/mcnair/vol15/iss1/10

Nagda, B., & Zúñiga, X. (2003). Fostering meaningful racial engagement through intergroup dialogues. *Group Processes & Intergroup Relations, 6*(1), 111–128. doi:10.1177/1368430203006001015

Orcher, L. (2005). *Conducting research: Social and behavioral science methods*. Glendale, CA: Pyrczak Publishing.

Oxford American Dictionary for Learner of English. (2011). Oxford, England, and New York, NY: Oxford University Press.

Parish, C. (1946). Color names and color notions. *Journal of Negro Education, 15*(1), 13–20.

Patterson, R. (2011). "Woman thou art bound": Critical spectatorship, Black masculine gazes, and gender problems in Tyler Perry's movies. *Black Camera, 3*(1), 9–30. doi:10.1353/blc.2011.0039

Peshkin, A. (1988). In search of subjectivity—One's own. *Educational Researcher, 17*(7), 17–21. doi:10.3102/0013189xo17007017

Poulos, C. N. (2009). *Accidental ethnography: An inquiry into family secrecy*. Walnut Creek, CA: Left Coast Press.

Richardson, L. (2000). Evaluating ethnography. *Qualitative Inquiry, 6*(2), 253–255. doi:10.1177/107780040000600207

Russell, K., Wilson, M., & Hall, R. (1992). *The color complex: The politics of skin color among African Americas*. New York, NY: Random House, Inc.

Scanlon, J. (2007). "If my husband calls I'm not here": The beauty parlor as real and representational female space. *Feminist Studies, 33*(2), 308–334.

Schwalbe, M. (2008). *The sociologically examined life—pieces of the conversation* (4th ed.). Boston, MA: McGraw-Hill Higher Education.

Shapiro, S. (2006). *Loosing heart: The moral and spiritual mis-education of Americas children*. Mahwah, NJ: Lawrence Erlbaum.

Sharp, M. D., Riera, J.-L., & Jones, S. (2012). Telling our stories: Using autoethnography to construct identities at the intersections. *Journal of Student Affairs Research and Practice, 49*(3), 315–322. doi:10.1515/jsarp-2012-6338.

Simon, B., Aufderheide, B., & Kampmeier, C. (2008). The social psychology of minority-majority relations. In R. Brown & S. L. Gaertner (Eds.), *Blackwell handbook of social psychology: Intergroup processes* (pp. 303–323). Oxford, UK: Blackwell Publishers Ltd.

Sniderman, P., & Piazza, T. (1993). *The scar of race*. United States of America: President and Fellows of Harvard College.

Speight, S. (2006). Internalized racism: One more piece of the puzzle. *The Counseling Psychologist, 207*(35), 126-134. doi:10.11777/0011000006295119

Story, J. (2006). *Cultural theory and popular culture an introduction*. Athens, GA: The University of Georgia Press.

Tate, S. (2007). Black beauty: Shade, hair and anti-racist aesthetics. *Ethnic and Racial Studies, 30*(2), 300-319. doi:10.1080/01419870601143992.

Tatum, B. D. (2000). The complexity of identity: "Who am I?" In M. Adams, W. J. Blumenfeld, R. Castaneda, H. W. Hackman, M. L. Peters, & X. Zúñiga (Eds.), *Readings for diversity and social justice: An anthology on racism, antisemitism, sexism, heterosexism, ableism, and classism* (pp. 9-14). New York, NY: Routledge.

Thompson, A. (2010). Tiffany, friend of people of color: White investments in anti-racism. *International Journal of Qualitative Studies in Education, 16*(1), 7-29. doi:10.1080/0951839032000033509

Thompson, C., & Carter, R. (1997). *Racial identity theory: Applications to individual, group, and organizational interventions*. Mahwah, NJ: Lawrence Erlbaum.

Wertz, F., Charmaz, K., McMullen, L., Josselson, R., Anderson, R., & McSpadden, E. (2011). *Five ways of doing qualitative analysis: Phenomenological psychology, grounded theory, discourse analysis, narrative research and intuitive inquiry*. New York, NY: The Guilford Press.

West, C. (1995). Mammy, Sapphire and Jezebel: Historical images of Black women and their implications for psychotherapy. *Psychotherapy, 32*(3), 458-486.

West, C. (1999). *The Cornell West reader*. New York, NY: Basic Civitas Books.

West, C. (2001). *Race matters*. New York, NY: Vintage Books.

White, D. (1999). *Ar'n't I a woman? Female salves in the plantation south*. New York: Basic Books.

Wilder, J., & Cain, C. (2010). Teaching and learning color consciousness in Black families: Exploring family processes and women's experiences with colorism. *Journal of Family Issues 2011, 32*, 577. doi:10.1177/0192513X10390858

Williams, A. (2013). *BET Honors 2013 Recognizes Bishop TD Jakes*. Retrieved from http://breathecast.christianpost.com/articles/6184/20130211/bishop-td-jakes-bet-honors-2013-td-jakes-potterhouse-bishop-td-bishop-jakes-bet-music-awards.htm

Williams, M. (2006). The "crisis" cover girl: Lena Horne, the NAACP, and representations of African American femininity, 1941-1945. *American periodicals, 16*(2), 200-218.

Williams, M. (2009). "Meet the real Lena Horne": Representations of Lena Horne in *Ebony* magazine, 1945-1949. *Journal of American Studies, 43*(1), 117-130. doi:1017/SOO21875809006094

Williams, M., Teasdale, J., Segal, Z., & Kabat-Zinn, J. (2007). *The mindful way through depression: Freeing yourself from chronic unhappiness.* New York: Guilford Press.

Woodard, J., & Mastin, T. (2005). Black womanhood: Essence and its treatment of stereotypical images of Black women. *Journal of Black Studies, 26,* 264–281. doi:10.1177/0021934704273152

Young, M. (2000). Five faces of oppression. In M. Adams, W. J. Blumenfeld, R. Castaneda, H. W. Hackman, M. L. Peters, & X. Zuniga (Eds.), *Readings for diversity and social justice: An anthology on racism, antisemitism, sexism, heterosexism, ableism, and classism* (pp. 35–49). New York, NY: Routledge.

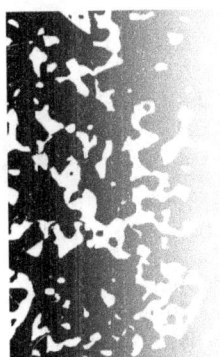

# INDEX

## A

African American community 12
African-American women,
  portrayal of 36-7 (see also
  stereotypes of Black women)
  exploitation of 16
  internalized racism within 21
  racial profiling 18-19
  unjust killings of 19
Allison, Dr 66-7
authentic Blackness, idea of 55
authenticity 10
autoethnography 8-9

## B

Bell, Derrick 18
Berry, Halle 40-1
Beyoncé 44
Black Feminist Thought (BFT) 7, 35, 41-2
Black Lives Matter Movement 18
Black nationalism 24
Blackness 2, 22, 26, 55, 63-5, 67, 78-9, 84-5, 90
Bonilla-Silva, Eduardo 18
brown-skinned Black women 39

## C

Campbell, Tisha 47
childhood fights 1-4, 12
chronic disorder 4
civil rights movement 15, 24, 81
collective identity of Black
  women 8, 42, 88; see also
  stereotypes of Black women
Collins, Patricia Hill 34
color-blind racism 18
colorism 4-8, 30, 52, 74-5
  Alpha Kappa Alpha
    woman 58-61
  amongst men 69-70
  in college campus 66
  color stratification in church
    setting 61-3
  Delta Sigma Theta woman 61
  description of a real
    sistah 65-7
  different meanings of 80
  discrimination and 71
  divisiveness based on skin
    tone 24-6
  early stages of 22-3
  education, importance of 80-6

effects of 6, 12
gendered 26
healing 80
idea of telling a story about 57
intra social effects of 9
*intra* turmoil 29
media representations 84-6
passing for white 23-4
reaffirming and transformative 28
relationship with children 55-7
self-actualization of Blackness 63-7
sense within family 53-63
skin color bias 21
stereotypes of 85
#teamlightskin 72-3
terminology 21-2
trauma of 71-2
color stratification 7, 77-8
in church setting 61-3
Critical Race Theory (CRT) 7, 29
core principles of 17-19
cultural imperialism 19-20
culturally relevant education 82-4

**D**
*Dark Girls* (Berry and Duke) 6
dark-skinned Black girls 29, 37, 67, 69
Davis, Viola 39
discrimination 71, 76
DIVAS 70-1
*Don't Play in the Sun* (Golden) 28
*Down with Fraggle Rock* 9
*Dream Girls* 39
Dubois, W. E. B. 15
Dyers, Richard 16

**E**
education, importance of 80-6, 89
culturally relevant education 82-4
educational knowledge 52
Emancipation Proclamation 16

**F**
*Fences* 39
field negro 76

film industry 36-7
Freire, Paulo 83, 89

**G**
gendered colorism 26
*Ghost* 38
Goldberg, Whoopi 38, 45
Golden, Marita 79-80
*Gone With the Wind* 37-8

**H**
*Hallelujah* 39
hegemony 19-20
*The Help* 38
Historically Black College/University (HBCU) 66
Horne, Lena 39, 44
house negro 75
Hudson, Jennifer 38

**I**
Imes-James, Monique 39
industrial times 15
intergroup dialogue (IGD) 86-7
internalized racism 4-8, 20-1, 75, 78, 81-2, 88-9
inter-racism 4
intra-racism 4-5, 8

**J**
Jakes, Bishop T. D. 85
*A Jazzman's Blues* 85
jezebel image of Black woman 39-41, 43-4, 48, 84
journaling 87-8

**K**
Kantor, Jody 44
King, Jr., Martin Luther 13

**L**
Lee, Spike 45, 47-8
light-skinned Black man 77
light-skinned Black women 7, 24, 29, 40, 44, 47, 66, 85
challenges of 2-4
collective identity of 45
quality of life 5
Limbaugh, Rush 44
Lincoln, Abraham 16

# INDEX

## M
*Malcolm X* 41
mammy image of Black woman 37–9, 43
marginalized group 7, 12, 21
    negative ideas about 20
marriage 27
McDaniel, Hattie 37–8, 42
McKinney, Nina Mae 39
*Monster's Ball* 40–1

## N
narrative inquiry 28
National Association for the Advancement of Colored People (NAACP) 37
Njeri, Itabari 26

## O
Obama, Barack 18
Obama, Michelle 43
O'Brian, Soledad 64, 78

## P
paper bag test 24–5, 54
Parrish, Charles 21
passing for white 23–4
Perry, Tyler 84–5
plantation life 15
popular culture 35, 89
*Precious* 39
Predominately White Institution (PWI) 65

## R
race and racism 4, 6, 51, 89
    basis of skin color 21
    biological evidence 14–15
    construction of 13–14, 16–17
    definition 13
    education, importance of 80–6
    evolution of 18
    material benefits 19
    modern-day 18–19
    race relations 15–16
    skin tone value in 12
Ray, James Earl 13
reaffirming 28
right color skin 7

## S
sapphire image of Black woman 38–9, 43
*School Daze* 45–8
    Alpha Kappa Alpha Sorority, Inc. (AKA) 46, 48, 58–61
    beauty salon scene 46
    Delta Sigma Theta Sorority, Inc. (DST) 46, 61
    Gamma Phi Gamma 46
    Jigaboos 46, 58
    process of pledging 46–7
    traces of colorism 46
    Wannabes 46, 48, 58
self-actualization of Blackness 63–7
self-healing 5
share cropping 15
slave trade 15–16
    abolition of slavery 16
social identity 34
social values 34
soul drive-bys 25
*Sparkle* 85
Spencer, Octavia 38
stereotypes of Black women 36–7
    jezebel 39–41
    mammy 37–8
    reality and 43–4
    sapphire 38–9
Stevens, Sapphire 38

## T
#teamBlack 73
#teamlightskin 72–3
Thornton, Billy Bob 40
*Training Day* 41
transformative colorism 28
Tyler Perry Studios 85

## V
victimization 75

## W
Washington, Denzel 41
*Who is Black in America?* 78–9
Williams, M. 44
Williams, Tammy 85
World War I (1914–1918) 15
wrong color 6

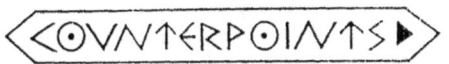

## Studies in Criticality

*General Editor*
*Shirley R. Steinberg*

Counterpoints publishes the most compelling and imaginative books being written in education today. Grounded on the theoretical advances in criticalism, feminism, and postmodernism in the last two decades of the twentieth century, Counterpoints engages the meaning of these innovations in various forms of educational expression. Committed to the proposition that theoretical literature should be accessible to a variety of audiences, the series insists that its authors avoid esoteric and jargonistic languages that transform educational scholarship into an elite discourse for the initiated. Scholarly work matters only to the degree it affects consciousness and practice at multiple sites. Counterpoints' editorial policy is based on these principles and the ability of scholars to break new ground, to open new conversations, to go where educators have never gone before.

For additional information about this series or for the submission of manuscripts, please contact:

> Shirley R. Steinberg, General Editor
> msgramsci@gmail.com

To order other books in this series, please contact our Customer Service Department:

> peterlang@presswarehouse.com (within the U.S.)
> orders@peterlang.com (outside the U.S.)

Or browse online by series:

> www.peterlang.com

www.ingramcontent.com/pod-product-compliance
Lightning Source LLC
Chambersburg PA
CBHW061720300426
44115CB00014B/2761